TOUGH LOVE

TOUCHED
BY AN
ANGEL

TOUGH LOVE

Story and teleplay by DEL SHORES

MARTHA WILLIAMSON,
EXECUTIVE PRODUCER

Novelization by ROBERT TINE

Based on the television series created by
JOHN MASIUS

THOMAS NELSON PUBLISHERS
Nashville

Published in Nashville, Tennessee, by Thomas Nelson, Inc.,
Publishers.

   Library of Congress Cataloging-in-Publication Data
Tine, Robert.
    Tough love / story and teleplay, Del Shores; Martha
  Williamson, executive producer; novelization by Robert Tine;
  based on the television series by John Masius.
      p.   cm.
    ISBN 0-7852-7131-7 (pbk.)
    1. Shores, Del. II. Touched by an angel (Television
  program). III. Title.
PS3570.I48T68 1999
813'.54—dc21   98-50579
                                                          CIP

           Printed in the United States of America
           1 2 3 4 5 6 QPK 04 03 02 01 00 99

Chapter One

$\mathcal{M}$onica and Tess sat at a well laid out table, set down in the middle of a forest glade, overhung by the branches of a dozen gnarled trees and surrounded by the lull of a quiet stream. They were alone in the forest as far as they knew, seated at the only table around for miles, and neither angel seemed to think it unusual. In fact, they had not taken any notice of their surroundings, as they were engaged in a very serious discussion.

There was a vast world of knowledge that an angel like Monica could learn from a more experienced angel like Tess. Monica was new at casework, and she never tired of listening to her supervisor. Tess, with her long centuries of knowledge, skills, and training, had much to pass on to her colleague. But that morning the topic of conversation was, of all things . . . coffee.

"Oh, this smells wonderful, Tess," said Monica. "Really wonderful." She breathed in the steam rising from the cup, but something seemed to be holding her back from actually tasting the coffee.

It was a reluctance that Tess was not slow to notice. "Honey," she said gently, "will you stop just *smelling* the coffee?" Tess shook her head slowly. "Sooner or later you've got to drink it, you know. It's like life . . ."

"Like life, Tess?"

"That's right," Tess replied, nodding. "You never really know how good it is until you go on and taste it. All coffee doesn't taste the same, just as no two lives are exactly alike. That much should be easy to figure out."

Tess handed a tiny cup to Monica, who inhaled the aroma rising from it. "See, that's espresso. Nothing more than a little bit of hot water and a lot of coffee."

"Smells strong," said Monica.

"That's right, strong and bitter. Some people like it like that. Rich and undiluted."

"Sounds tempting," said Monica. She took a tentative peek at the cup of espresso, but still didn't drink.

Tess laughed quietly. "Oh, it's tempting all right. Very tempting, Miss Wings . . . But there's another side to an espresso kind of life . . . You know what that is?"

Monica shook her head.

"Heartburn!" Tess announced.

Monica giggled. "Really?"

"Believe it. Heartburn is the price you pay for all that flavor."

Monica laughed again. "You make espresso sound so downright dangerous," she said. "As if it's not to be trusted."

3

"Well, my choice of coffee is not espresso or any of those newfangled flavors they have around these days."

"No?" Monica asked. "What's your choice?"

"For my money, there is nothing like a good ol' cup of Joe." She raised her coffee cup. "No camouflage . . . when you try to hide what's deep down, underneath, you just end up feeling miserable." As she sipped her coffee, a white dove flew out of the sky and settled on the edge of the table.

Monica and Tess looked down at the small bird. "Well, what are you doing here?" Monica asked. But both angels knew why the dove was there . . .

In an instant the forest glade was gone; and Tess and Monica, still seated at the same table, found themselves on the terrace of a restaurant in the center of a large city. It was lunchtime and the place was packed, but no one had given the new arrivals so much as a second glance.

"Monica," said Tess soberly, "you're about to meet a woman who doesn't know how to deal with something as simple as a plain cup of ordinary Joe."

Monica looked around the terrace. At one table sat two men earnestly discussing their golf games. At another a circle of elderly women traded pictures of grandchildren as if they were playing some new card game. At a third table were a young woman and her seven-year-old daughter, the two of them giggling over a shared joke. Monica frowned.

"I'm sorry," she said, a bit mystified. "I can't tell who you are talking about, Tess."

Tess glanced toward the mother and daughter sitting at the shaded table in the corner.

"I found him!" said the little girl happily, pointing to an elephant in her picture book.

With a look of mock astonishment, the young

woman said, "I don't believe it! You are so smart! You found him." She reached over, gave the little girl a hug and gently tickled her. The girl's squeals and giggles were evidence that the two of them were thoroughly enjoying their time together.

Monica was not given to doubting Tess, but these two didn't appear to be in need of any angelic assistance.

"One of *them*?" Monica asked incredulously. She looked back at the pair. "But they seem so very happy, Tess."

"Seem . . . ," said Tess. "Sure they *seem* happy. A lot of people *seem* happy. I would have thought you'd have learned by now that the truth is never that simple." She shook her head, then looked back at the table. "Believe me, those are not happy people."

As Monica followed her gaze, an attractive, middle-aged woman emerged from inside the restaurant and paused in the doorway, making an entrance. She was a tall, fashionable woman with dark eyes and a definite sense of command.

But Monica picked up something else—the woman's eyes were glazed and she seemed a little unsteady on her feet.

"I made it!" she announced. Her words were slurred and her voice was a little too loud. Diners looked up from their plates, and conversations broke off; all eyes turned to the woman in the doorway.

"I made it!" she repeated, louder this time. "Look who's finally here! Happy birthday, Baby!"

The woman threw her arms open wide. As she did so, her outstretched arms collided with the waiter who stood behind her holding a beautifully decorated birthday cake. The cake slammed into the waiter's chest, squashing the frosting, and chunks of cake flew everywhere. She turned to the waiter. "Why don't you watch where you're going, Mister?"

The little girl's mother rose halfway from the table. "Oh, Mother! Please . . . you promised me . . ."

Only the little girl took it all in stride. She

giggled when she saw her grandmother smack the cake into the waiter's chest.

In a matter of seconds, a perfectly peaceful restaurant had become a shambles. And in the same instant, Monica got a better understanding of her new assignments.

Tess turned and looked at Monica. "Any questions?"

Chapter Two

Elizabeth Jessup's front yard had seen better days. It had once been a lush green lawn stretching from the white steps at the front door to the colorful flower beds that lined the fence. The lawn was overgrown now and riddled with thick tangles of crabgrass. The sunflowers in the flower bed were dying, their stalks dried out, the petals drooping from lack of water. The once-ornamental fence that bordered the yard was now rusty and warped.

Jessup herself—the lady who had so efficiently ruined her granddaughter's birthday lunch at

9

the restaurant just the day before—was floundering in the untidy garden. Her feet had become entangled in a piece of metal that framed the flower bed, and she was working—with little success—to free herself.

"Oh great," Elizabeth muttered as she thrashed around in the flowers. "I said, get out of the way . . . Out, I said."

Monica, who was making her way slowly down the street, saw this display of undignified behavior. Sadly, she knew there had been a time, not long ago, when this woman had stood in the forefront of American journalism as one of the most distinguished foreign correspondents of her day, which was quite an accomplishment. Not only was this considered a job for a man, but the few women who had managed to break into the old boys' club—famous women like Nelly Bly, Martha Gellhorn, and Janet Flanner—were all Caucasian. Elizabeth had two strikes against her: not only was she a woman, she was an *African-American* woman.

Elizabeth had set her sights on her goals early in life when she first discovered the excitement of reading a well-written news story. With her outgoing personality, a natural gift for writing, and a great deal of encouragement from one of her teachers, Elizabeth had decided even as a young student that she wanted to be a journalist. Not just a local news writer, but a full-fledged foreign correspondent, then considered the pinnacle of the profession.

Elizabeth knew it would not be easy. Her first job after college was as a lowly copy clerk for a small-town paper where she considered herself lucky if she was given an assignment to write the occasional obituary or weather report. But she was determined to stick with it until she managed to parlay her humble copy job into a full-time writing position. She covered every inch of her little town. There wasn't a quilting bee or a bake-off, a petty theft, a car accident, or a middle-school graduation that she did not cover. And while the work was far from glamorous, and although Elizabeth's store of patience was not noticeably deep, she stayed on and did her job conscientiously and with painstaking care. When she wasn't banging out a story on a local fire or writing up the police blotter, she hung out in the newsroom, listening to the older hack journalists—the stories they would tell, the tips of the trade they would impart, the names they would mention . . . young Elizabeth listened to it all, and soaked it up like a sponge.

When the workday was done, it was not unusual to move the conversation to the old tavern across the street. At first, Elizabeth did not take a drink, preferring to stick to iced tea or ginger ale. But under the good-natured cajoling of the other journalists, who were mostly men, she took her first sips of alcohol to fit in. The courage and determination she gained in her daily fight for newsworthy articles often became lost in her deep desire to be accepted by the other reporters. In time, she came to develop a liking for the drinks they offered.

Monica knew the bare details of this story when she came face-to-face with Elizabeth, but she did not really know the mumbling woman smashing around in her beat-up sunflowers.

Monica announced herself. "Hello," she said. "Good morning."

Elizabeth looked up and scowled at her. "What do you want?" she asked gruffly.

"Are you Elizabeth Jessup?" Monica asked. "I'm looking for Ms. Jessup."

Elizabeth stood up to her full height and put a fist on each hip. "Am I Elizabeth Jessup? Who wants to know?" Without waiting for a reply, she returned to the task at hand, ignoring Monica completely. She was determined to get out of that tangle of old wire and dead plants if it was the last thing she did.

But Monica watched as Elizabeth managed to make the tangle even worse. "May I help you?" she asked in her comforting brogue. "Perhaps I can give you a hand there, Ms. Jessup."

"I don't need any help," Elizabeth said. As

she spoke, a piece of the wire shot up, sending her reeling, but releasing her from captivity. "See," she said. "No help needed."

"You're sure?" Monica asked.

Elizabeth stood straight again and brushed the wrinkles from her red silk blouse. Peering at Monica closely, she could tell there was more to this woman than the casual concern of a passerby. It was a moment before she spoke.

"What is it you want, exactly? And who are you, by the way?"

"My name is Monica," the angel replied.

"That's nice," said Elizabeth. She wondered if she knew this young woman from someplace and had forgotten all about meeting her. That was happening more and more these days. It could be very embarrassing.

"I understand you are writing your memoirs, and I—"

"Now who told you that?" she asked abruptly.

"Your publisher," said Monica quickly. "And I have been engaged to help you finish them."

"*You?*" Elizabeth asked. "You are going to write *my* memoirs? How do you plan on doing that? You weren't there. They're not your memories . . . and besides, I never use ghostwriters. I have been writing my whole life. You'd think that awful publisher of mine would at least have some faith that I can get them written."

"No, no," said Monica. "I wouldn't be writing them exactly." Monica knew that a little hand-holding would not hurt the situation. "Of course, no one could do that but you, Ms. Jessup."

"That's right," said Elizabeth vehemently. "My memories. *My* memoirs."

"Absolutely," Monica agreed, equally emphatic. "Yours and yours alone."

"And don't you forget it," said Elizabeth. "But that does not answer the question." She peered at Monica again. "Just how are you going to help me?"

"Oh," said Monica, "That's simple. I have been sent along as a sort of secretary. I'll take dictation, I'll do the typing . . . anything you need."

"Well, Monica . . ." Elizabeth's voice was suddenly light and pleasant. "You're young so you might not know it, but I have never had a deadline in my entire career as a journalist that I did not make. I once had to turn in a story in Saigon written on the back of my last clean T-shirt. Hmm? Understand?"

"Yes, but—"

Then, suddenly, without warning, Elizabeth's voice turned cold. "So you can go back and tell that pathetic publisher that Elizabeth Jessup has never missed a deadline. Understand me?"

The truth of it was, Elizabeth's memoirs were giving her a certain amount of trouble, which she was extremely reluctant to face up to. To have trouble writing anything was a definite blow to her considerable pride. She had always been self-satisfied with her ability to make a deadline, to hit the mark every time. Even now she knew that given a collection of notes and a couple of quotes she could bang out a straight news story in a matter of minutes. Give her an hour or two and she would be able to write a piece of fluid, lucid political analysis that would neatly sum up the doings in the nation's capital or the state of foreign affairs.

It was with her own life—the examination of her own motives and actions—that Elizabeth had trouble. Still, she could not bring herself to admit that she had problems.

"You still here?" she said to Monica after a moment or two of total silence.

She looked at Monica for a second, glowering at her, hoping she could burn her message into Monica's memory. Then she turned and walked up the cracked concrete path toward the house. As far as she was concerned, the conversation was over. In truth, she was a little offended that her publisher, for whom she had written a half dozen best-selling books over the years and who had practically *begged* her to write her memoirs, had sent this young girl to help her with her work. Her editor had never asked if she needed the assistance. But here was this girl, all ready to pitch in and become her secretary. It was not, she decided, a vote of confidence. And Elizabeth's confidence was a little shaky these days—not that she would have ever admitted it to anyone, least of all to herself.

"How dare they!" she muttered to herself as she walked up the path toward the house.

But Monica, of course, could not let it end there. She threw open the sagging iron gate and rushed after her.

"Ms. Jessup, your manuscript was due at your publisher's more than two months ago. They are getting a little antsy about it. That is why they sent me."

"Let them get antsy," Elizabeth retorted. "I don't care if they have a whole ant colony in their pants."

She kept right on marching toward the house, not even bothering to turn her head. "And while we're on the subject, let me tell you something; that was *their* deadline. Understand? As far as I'm concerned I am right on schedule . . ."

"Now listen," Elizabeth ordered. "Before you leave"—(as if Monica's departure were a foregone conclusion)—"if you see a newspaper out front here somewhere, you let me know."

Monica looked puzzled. "Newspaper?"

"My morning delivery!" Elizabeth almost shouted as she looked around. "My paper is out here someplace—but who can tell where?"

"I don't see it," said Monica.

"Of course you don't," said Elizabeth, starting up an aluminum ladder that was leaning against the house. "See? It's the kids. The delivery kids. They don't care. They don't care where they throw the thing." She waved a hand at the roof. "Up, down, on the porch, through the window . . ."

She was climbing the ladder with surprising nimbleness and grace. "Most of the time it ends up right here on the roof. I can't tell you how many times I've had to haul out this ladder and climb up here just to get my morning paper."

Despite the ease with which Elizabeth climbed, Monica was not at all sure she should be up there.

"Can I *help* you?" she asked again.

Elizabeth turned. "What is this," she asked, "your first big break or something? Hmm? Is that it? You sit at the feet of a legendary journalist and one day you sit down and write your own book and you figure you have the right to call yourself my protége. Is that what this is all about?"

Monica laughed. "Sorry to disillusion you, but you're not *that* legendary."

For a moment it looked as if Elizabeth was going to take offense, then she smiled broadly and did an adequate imitation of Monica's voice: "'*Not that legendary,' she says . . .*"

As she laughed she pushed off the roof of the house and for a second or two the ladder wobbled in midair. Monica grabbed the base and steadied it, preventing the ladder and Elizabeth from crashing to the ground.

Monica had a firm grasp on the ladder, but Elizabeth did not have a firm grip on the roof. "Would you still like me to leave," Monica asked innocently, ". . . or should I stay for a while?"

Monica held the ladder as Elizabeth climbed down. The older woman seemed a little less cocky than she had before—her arrogance having been tempered by the fact that Monica had just prevented a horrible accident. She was almost nice as she led the pretty, auburn-haired girl into the house, and she suddenly became more open to the idea of assistance.

The interior was as drab as the outside and every square inch of surface space was covered with heaps of books and sheaves of papers. Hanging on the walls were dozens of dusty framed pictures of Elizabeth with famous people, as well as plaques and awards.

"Well," said Elizabeth, "this is sort of a trial run, you understand, because I don't really need any help . . . but if it gets you a paycheck I guess you could stick around for a while . . . I know what it's like to need the money."

"Thank you," Monica replied.

"Want a drink?" Elizabeth asked.

Monica's face brightened. "Oh," she said, "I'd

love a cup of nonfat decaf mocha latte with a little powdered nutmeg on the side." As she spoke a dreamy look came into her eyes as though she could almost taste the invigorating brew. (Tess had obviously taught her an awful lot about coffee in a very short time.) Elizabeth looked at her as if she were crazy

"What do you think I'm running here?" she asked. "A branch of Starbucks?"

Monica was not quite sure what Starbucks was, but instantly realized that she had asked for too much. "A cup of Joe would be just fine, Ms. Jessup."

"A cup of Joe," Elizabeth repeated with some surprise. "I haven't heard coffee called a cup of Joe since I was in the newsroom of the *Herald Tribune*—the one in New York," she added, "not that skinny little paper they put out in Paris." Elizabeth was extremely particular about her journalistic bona fides.

"Now," she continued, "if you want a drink, I have a nice pitcher of cold iced tea. I made it myself," she said evenly. "It's a secret family recipe."

Monica looked a little puzzled. The iced tea sounded delicious, but she hesitated about accepting it. "Well . . . I haven't worked my way up to tea yet, but how about some water?"

"Water?" said Elizabeth, turning toward the kitchen. "You sure I can't interest you in a glass of iced tea? I usually take a glass of it myself at this time of the morning."

"Water will be just fine, thanks . . . ," said Monica, wondering why Elizabeth was making such a fuss over her iced tea. She made a mental note to ask Tess about tea the next time they met.

"So, what are your qualifications?" Elizabeth called from the kitchen. "Or are you one of those English lit majors from some tony Ivy League school who never dirtied her hands with short-hand and touch typing? Those are the kind of girls publishers love to hire. They just want to be in the book business and they don't want much money—they all have trust funds."

Monica laughed. "That's not me you're describing, Ms. Jessup. I do know shorthand and I can type like the blazes. You'll find I'm quite useful."

"Really? Will I? Well, for starters, can you take dictation? That would be a big help." Elizabeth removed a large pitcher from the refrigerator.

"Yes," Monica called back. "I take dictation perfectly. And I'm really fast at that too."

"Good. I can tell you're not the Ivy League type. They don't teach those kinds of skills at Yale. Maybe they teach the philosophy of typing, but I doubt if they teach the real thing. I never went to college. Didn't need to."

She put some ice in a glass and filled it with water. "How about research skills? I might send you out to the library and the newspaper morgues to do some research."

As Elizabeth spoke, Monica ventured into the living room to study a series of black-and-white pictures leaning on the mantel above the fireplace: one showed Elizabeth waist-deep in jungle mud, another caught her in full camouflage crouching behind a ruined wall while a squad of soldiers fired on an unseen foe.

There were impressive photos of her with various world leaders—every American president since Johnson, a brace of British prime ministers, and a half dozen African leaders in national dress. Then Monica noticed a series of pictures that had the same basic theme. There was Elizabeth with her fellow journalists: packed into restaurant booths, gathered at bars, sitting around café tables . . . all of them raising a glass to the camera. But one photograph did not fit in with the rest. In it Elizabeth posed with the young woman Monica had seen her with at the restaurant the day before, her daughter, Sydney. The young woman wore a graduation gown and both women had the same look on their faces: happiness mixed with deep pride.

Elizabeth emerged from the kitchen, a glass of water in one hand, a glass of pale brown iced tea in the other. "I'm a stickler for details, you know," she said. "It's my trademark."

"I know," said Monica. Just then the phone rang, but as Monica reached for the receiver, Elizabeth sprinted across the room to stop her.

"No. No! Don't answer that!" Elizabeth insisted. "Do not touch that phone. I forbid it!"

"But . . . but why not?"

"I've been getting a lot of prank calls recently," said Elizabeth. "The more you answer, the more likely they are to call. Leave it alone so they'll get bored and give it up."

Monica smiled. "Don't worry, I can handle it," she said as she picked up the phone. "Hello. This is Monica." Elizabeth leaned in, trying to find out who was on the other end. "I've just been hired as Ms. Jessup's new assistant," Monica continued. This piece of information evoked a moment of silence on Monica's end as whoever was calling peppered her with questions. "Yes," she said finally. "It happened just like that. It was actually the suggestion of her publisher. So they sent me to help her. We're getting along like a house on fire."

Elizabeth rolled her eyes and took a deep gulp of her iced tea.

"Ah, certainly," said Monica. "Would you hold on for a moment please?" She covered the mouthpiece of the phone with her hand and turned to Elizabeth.

"It's your daughter," Monica said. "And she wants to know what time you want them to come over."

"Come over?" said Elizabeth, giving Monica a puzzled look. "Come over for what?"

"I think you invited them over for dinner," Monica replied. "For tonight."

Elizabeth's face fell. "Oh yeah . . . I forgot about that. Yesterday was my granddaughter's birthday and some idiot waiter dropped the cake . . ." At least, that was how *Elizabeth* remembered it. "And I suggested that they come over tonight so we could try again, but, ah . . ."

The invitation had completely slipped her mind. She had not bought any food—she hadn't even prepared a menu—the house was a mess and as for her granddaughter's birthday cake, she hadn't even given it a thought. Not that she was much of a cook or a baker at the best of times. Besides, she felt horrible.

She took another drink of her iced tea. "You know, Monica, tell her that tonight is not good. In fact, let's put it off until—"

But Monica ignored the instructions of her new employer. "How about eight o'clock?" she said. "That's great. We'll see you then. Bye-bye." She hung up and smiled at Elizabeth. "How's that? It'll be fun, don't you think?"

Elizabeth frowned and drained her glass. She was not happy about this development, but it was plain that she could not avoid this particular *fait accompli*. "I think we better get in gear and go shopping," said Elizabeth. "That's what I think . . ."

There was a large farmer's market not far from Elizabeth's house and the two women spent an hour there stocking up on the ingredients they would need for their dinner. As they made their way from stall to stall, testing the wares, Elizabeth did most of the talking. She complained about professional slights real and imagined, professional rivalries, personalities famous and infamous; but she reserved most of her venom for her own daughter, Sydney.

"Make sure you buy lots of fruits and vegetables," said Monica. "Greens make you healthy."

"You haven't even met Sydney and already you're talking like her," said Elizabeth.

Monica picked up a bunch of beautiful white roses. "These will make a lovely centerpiece," she said, showing Elizabeth the flowers. "Don't you think?"

"Yeah, whatever," said Elizabeth, hardly looking at the flowers. "That's just the kind of thing Sydney would say. Like I said, you could be sisters."

"She sounded lovely on the phone this afternoon," Monica replied. "Really, she did."

"Sure, she sounds lovely to you, Monica," Elizabeth responded sharply. "But that's only because you haven't met her yet." She held up a red apple and examined it with the concentration of a jeweler examining a ruby.

"Come on," Monica protested. "She can't be *that* bad. You make her sound like a horror."

Elizabeth put the apple back on the pile. "The child has been contrary since the day she was born," she said bitterly. She stopped and faced Monica head-on. "And I might add she was born at the most inconvenient moment possible."

"When was that?" Monica asked.

"Just as the Six-Day War was about to begin . . . Here you had one of the great stories of the century on the verge of breaking. Israel takes on the entire Arab world: Egypt, Jordan, Syria—all of them. Israel doesn't just win, she pounds the tar out of them and does it in less than a week. And I missed it!" Elizabeth still felt the pain of not being part of that piece of history.

"What happened?"

"I had to have a baby, that's what happened," Elizabeth replied. "I was on my way to Israel from New York. Went into labor in London and my bureau chief turns me around and sends me right back to the United States to have her. I told him I'd give birth in Israel, take a day to recuperate, and that way I could cover the rest of the war—of course we didn't know the war was going to be so brief."

"Of course not," said Monica. "You would have no way of knowing that."

"Everyone thought it was going to be a knock-down-drag-out fight that would go on for months, maybe even years . . ." Elizabeth sighed. "So I didn't protest. I got back on the flight, flew home to the States, and had Sydney. I didn't get back to Israel until day seven. The war was over. Wouldn't you know it?"

The look on Monica's face softened. "But a

baby," she said. "Surely, a baby is more grand than any newspaper assignment ever could be."

"That is the kind of attitude that marks you as a great mother and an absolutely lousy journalist, young lady," Elizabeth announced.

"I'm sure *you're* both," said Monica. "And I'll bet Sydney would agree with me."

"If I were you I would reserve judgment until you meet her," Elizabeth said. "She takes no risks, she has no fire . . . the girl's picture is next to Milquetoast in the dictionary."

"Oh, Elizabeth," said Monica, "that's a terrible thing to say about your own daughter."

"No," Elizabeth protested, "I'm serious. Sydney and I have only one thing in common."

"See," said Monica triumphantly. "You do have a common bond."

Elizabeth nodded. "Right. And it is the wrong kind of bond. We both have terrible taste in men."

"Oh," said Monica. She always felt as if she were on shaky ground when relations between men and women came up. "How is that?"

Elizabeth continued. "We just can't pick the right men. Her man died on her, and me, I just wore mine out." This seemed to bother her for a moment, then, as if changing gears she launched into another subject.

"Hey, have I told you about the time I went with President Nixon to China back in '72?" Elizabeth seemed to have forgotten that Monica had only started working for her that morning and had heard none of the stories that would make up Elizabeth's journalistic memoirs. Monica thought it would be rude to point that out.

"No, you haven't told me," she said.

"Well, you remember how the whole thing started? With the Ping-Pong players going over to China . . . That got me thinking about the next move. We had isolated China for so long that to me the idea of something as trivial as Ping-Pong players being the reason for a presidential visit meant there *had* to be something bigger going on. So I started calling around . . ."

Monica could see that Elizabeth was off—that

smile on her face that suggested she preferred to live in the glorious past rather than the dull and inconvenient present.

Chapter Three

When Monica and Elizabeth returned to the Jessup house after the afternoon's shopping, Elizabeth grabbed a cold pitcher of iced tea from the refrigerator and announced that she would be working in her study for a while.

"That's fine," said Monica. "I can manage the dinner and the cake, of course."

"No," Elizabeth announced. "Baking is one thing I will be able to do without assistance. You'll have plenty to do, Monica. You leave the birthday cake to me."

Monica nodded. "As you wish . . . You're the boss around here, you know."

"And don't you forget it," said Elizabeth. "There are a lot of editors who forgot that, and they ended up taking early retirement. Understand?"

"I'll keep it in mind."

Monica had learned quite a bit about kitchens and cooking from Tess, and it was not a difficult task to make a dinner for three adults and a child. There would be a simple but tasty dinner of grilled chicken with a sauté of fresh vegetables for an entrée and, of course, the birthday cake for dessert. Monica was so engrossed in the myriad of tasks at hand, she failed to notice the stillness in the house. If Elizabeth was a hard worker she was also a very quiet one.

Once dinner was well on its way to completion Monica set herself to the next task at hand: some secretarial work on Elizabeth Jessup's famous—and late—memoirs. She made her way through the house to the study. The room was so dark and stuffed with books and souvenirs that even though it was the middle of a sunny day, Monica had to turn on the overhead light and the goosenecked lamp on the oversize desk to light the room. She was surprised to find the room empty—if Elizabeth Jessup was working on her memoirs she was not working in the study.

Stacked on both sides of the stained blotter were pieces of the manuscript. On the left were pages written out in Elizabeth's small, but extremely neat handwriting. On the right was a pile of typed pages, each meticulously edited in red pencil by Elizabeth. In the middle of the blotter was a battered old typewriter. It seemed that Elizabeth was of the old school of journalists, the kind who thought that a sophisticated computer would never replace an old, reliable, black-enamel Underwood manual.

Monica smiled at the thought of Elizabeth using the old machine, defiantly sticking to her antiquated ways. She looked again at the two piles of paper. Both stacks stood hardly half an inch high—Elizabeth was seriously behind the deadline set by her publisher. At this rate the book would *never* be finished.

She picked up some of the typed pages and read the first few paragraphs:

There wasn't a journalist in the Middle East— foreigner, Jew, or Arab—who didn't know there was going to be a war sometime that summer. Israel and Syria had skirmished across their borders since late in the winter and into the early spring. I remember being in Tel Aviv when I heard that a group of Israeli tanks had actually crossed the border into Syria and had engaged in a full-pitched battle. The editor of the foreign desk called me from London and told me in no uncertain terms to get out and to get out now! He wanted me to miss the biggest event in the history of the Middle East since the founding of Israel!

By the way . . . have I mentioned I was nine months pregnant at the time?

Monica laughed out loud. She could picture Elizabeth waiting with the timing of a skilled comedian for the right moment to drop that last piece of information on her readers. She continued to read. To her surprise, Elizabeth's written account of the events of the Six-Day War was slightly at variance with the story she had been told earlier that day. Monica's brow furrowed as she read.

The basic facts were the same—Elizabeth had been ordered out of the troubled region just before the June 5 commencement of the war, but in contrast to what she had told Monica earlier, she wrote, *"Much as I wanted to be there, I was carrying something precious, something I valued above the excitement and thrill of my profession . . ."*

The story then returned to the facts as Elizabeth had related them a few hours earlier, up to this point:

You have to remember that this was back in the dark ages of women in the workplace—never mind women in the war zone. However, my bosses—all men, of course—figured I had delivered the baby and that it was time to get back to work. (Maternity leave? No such thing!) If I wanted to play the boys' game, I had to play by the boys' rules. I got six days leave and then left my little girl behind. I'll never forget that moment. Sydney was so small and helpless (never mind that my husband, who was going to take care of her, looked big and helpless) and I was leaving her. The guilt I felt at that moment was overwhelming—I had never hated my job before, in fact, I had gloried in it. I felt that it was me, that it was what I had been put on earth to do. But I hated it then. I went anyway. I couldn't afford to look weak . . .

Monica frowned as she read those last words. They went a long way toward explaining Elizabeth's turn of mind these days, thirty years after the historic events in the Middle East.

She picked up another sheaf of handwritten pages of the memoir. Glancing at them briefly, she discovered that they were a straightforward account of Elizabeth's educated guess back in 1971 that relations were about to change between the United States of America and Communist China—a scoop that had won her the Pulitzer prize, but had put her in the doghouse with the president because he believed that she had stolen some of his thunder.

I was never on the enemies' list—but I was certainly not on the list to accompany President Nixon to China. Henry Kissinger intervened on my behalf and I got on the press plane at the last minute. Of course, Sydney told all her friends at school that I was going to China with the president, but—you know how kids are—not one of them believed her. I don't think her teacher believed it either. Then the New York Times *published a picture of Nixon standing next to Chairman Mao in the Great Hall of the People and in the background you could just make me out. I was squinting at Chairman Mao—the truth of it was, I was trying to figure out if that was his real hair—the man had very strange hair when you saw it close up. Sydney cut out the picture and carried it to school in triumph. The first thing she said to me when I got back was "Mommy, I was so proud of you . . ." It's just the kind of moment you would trade your Pulitzer for, believe me.*

Monica sighed and spooled a piece of fresh typing paper into the typewriter and then began to work, quickly turning the handwritten manuscript pages into orderly typescript.

Late in the afternoon, as she was setting the table for dinner, Monica discovered a treasure trove of linens, china, and silver. Elizabeth might prefer to appear that she didn't care much about the finer things in life, but over the years, she had obviously gone out of her way to collect beautiful remembrances from the many places she had visited in the course of her long and varied career. There were delicate linens from Ireland, intricately worked lace place mats from Italy, silver from Germany, fine china from England. One rare, five-branched silver candelabra caught Monica's eye. She knew that the white candles and the white roses would look lovely on the table.

Elizabeth emerged from her bedroom around five o'clock, a glass of iced tea in her hand. She stopped and gazed at the exquisitely set dining table, each napkin folded just so.

"Monica," said Elizabeth. "Oh . . . Monica. This looks just so, well, beautiful." She put down her drink and picked up one of the gold and red rimmed dinner plates. "Where did you find this china? I haven't seen it since '75 when Henry Kissinger and his wife came to dinner."

"I found it in the back of your china cabinet,"

Monica said softly. "I hope you don't mind me using it."

With exaggerated care Elizabeth put the dinner plate back in its place. "Man, that Henry Kissinger. Could he *eat*. I was terrified that I was going to run out of food. Luckily, Nancy—that's his wife—eats like a bird. She's as thin as six o'clock." Elizabeth picked up her glass of tea. "Now there's something that should make a nice chapter in my memoirs, don't you think?"

"Lovely," said Monica.

Elizabeth's eyes had fallen on something else on the dining table. A sheaf of papers neatly typed and stapled together. They lay on the plate where Elizabeth would sit.

"What's this?" she asked as she picked up the papers.

"It's our conversation . . . ," said Monica. "The one we had today about your trip to China with President Nixon. I thought if you were working, I might as well do my part as well."

"You're kidding!" said Elizabeth with a laugh.

"You *have* been busy. My lousy publisher is getting value for his money—and I bet he isn't paying you much either."

"Money doesn't matter," said Monica. And it was the absolute truth.

"You say that now," Elizabeth said, looking over the papers Monica had typed that afternoon. "But it matters when you don't have any . . ." She smiled and read aloud from the manuscript. "'So there I am, standing on the Great Wall of China . . . and freezing my blooming bottom off.'" Elizabeth looked up and blinked. "My blooming bottom? I'm not sure I have ever in my life—until now—uttered the phrase 'my blooming bottom.'"

Monica smiled, but she shifted uneasily. "Well . . . I did do a wee bit of editing."

"So I see," said Elizabeth. As she drained the last of her iced tea, the doorbell chimed.

"They're here," said Elizabeth. Then she called out, "Coming!" She fanned the air with the edited pages of her memoirs. "Very nice, Monica. Very nice."

Sydney's little girl, Beth, burst through the front door of the house, followed at a more stately pace by a tall, young woman, whom Monica recognized from the photo on the mantelpiece and from the restaurant the day before.

Mother and daughter greeted each other cordially—but they seemed to Monica to be a little reserved. That was not the case when Elizabeth enfolded her granddaughter, Beth, in a tight bear hug. "Oh, there she is. My sweet girl. Oh, my baby . . ."

"Hi, Grandma," Beth chirped. Then she wriggled out of her grandmother's arms and paused only to allow her mother to snatch off her coat before dashing away. She went directly to a glass-fronted cupboard in the hallway that held knick-knacks that Elizabeth had collected in a dozen countries.

There were fans and jade from her stays in the Far East, African carvings, bits and pieces of ceramic she had picked up in Zurich, Paris, and Florence. But the one thing that always caught

Beth's eye was a simple little piece of porcelain that Elizabeth had picked up somewhere, a white and brown ceramic figure of an angel. The figure was really a small child with wings holding some kind of stringed instrument—guitar, banjo, lute, it was hard to tell—and was mounted on a wooden pedestal. There was a key set in the base. Beth cranked it a couple of times and out came a very simple, music-box version of the timeless hymn "Amazing Grace."

"My sweetie," said Elizabeth. "How she loves that music box. I don't even remember where I got it . . ."

Sydney was not interested in the music box. She looked over at Monica and smiled, a slightly reserved smile.

"Oh," she said. "You must be Monica."

"Hello, Sydney. It is so nice to meet you," Monica replied, shaking the woman's hand. "How are you?"

"Monica is my new assistant," Elizabeth announced proudly, as if the whole thing had been her idea. "I have just hired her to help me . . . and I have begged her to stay for dinner."

Sydney hesitated for a moment, then nodded a little reluctantly. "Good." She looked around. "The house looks so . . . I don't know . . . it looks so together." She did her best not to look or sound surprised.

"I was inspired," said Elizabeth. She headed for the kitchen. "Anybody want a drink?"

"Something smells good," Sydney remarked when her mother was safely out of earshot. "Mom hasn't cooked a real meal in years. Not that I can remember, anyway . . ."

Monica thought it best not to mention who had actually done the lion's share of the work around the house, including the cooking. Let Sydney think better of her mother.

"Anyone want a drink?" Elizabeth called again from the kitchen.

Sydney seemed to tense. "Not for me, Mom."

No one else wanted a drink, except Elizabeth, of course, who remained in the kitchen to make a fresh pitcher of iced tea. When she returned, Monica, Beth, and Sydney were already seated at the table.

Everyone was enjoying the home-cooked meal. And even Monica helped herself to seconds.

"So, Beth," said Monica, "I hear you had a very important birthday yesterday. You know that seven is a very important age, don't you?"

The little girl had brought the music box to the table and she nodded solemnly as she wound it up for the fourth or fifth time in a row. "Uh-huh," she said. "I know. Seven is when you get to learn how to really read. All by yourself."

"That's right," Monica agreed. "Well, your mother must be very proud of you."

Sydney beamed, her whole face lighting up as she looked at her daughter. "Oh, I am, I am. She's my very special girl." She threw her arms around Beth and squeezed her tight. "Aren't you my special girl, Beth?"

"Yup," said Beth.

Elizabeth poured herself another glass of iced

tea. It was her second pitcher of the evening and she waved it at the rest of them as she queried, "Anyone else?"

Beth's hand shot up, like an eager student. "I want some, Grandma! Please!"

Elizabeth shook her head. "Uh-uh. Oh, dear, you're far too young for iced tea."

"But I'm seven now!" Beth protested.

Elizabeth nodded. "I know. That's what I mean . . ." She fumbled with a pack of cigarettes on the table, extracted one and lit it, exhaling a heavy stream of smoke.

Sydney frowned at the pall of blue smoke and tried to discreetly wave it away from where Beth was sitting. Elizabeth was oblivious to her daughter's discomfort.

"Now where was I?" said Elizabeth, enthusiastically smoking her cigarette. "Where was I . . . Ah yes, Paris. God, I love Paris . . . I used to spend a lot of time in Paris. It's the R&R station if you've been doing any work in the Middle East or North Africa . . ."

"What's R&R?" Beth asked.

"Rest and recreation," Elizabeth said. "Though I don't know how much rest anyone got back in the old days." She nudged Monica suggestively in the ribs. "Know what I mean, Monica?"

Monica didn't really know what she meant.

"One day I'm going to take you to Paris, Bethie. And we'll stroll the Champs Elysée together and eat *croque monsieur* at midnight on the banks of the Seine . . ."

"What's *croque monsieur*?" Beth asked.

Elizabeth took another deep drag on her cigarette. "Believe it or not," she said, "it's a nice way of saying grilled ham-and-cheese sandwich!"

Beth didn't notice her mother's discomfort, but she was enchanted by her grandmother and the stories of Paris. She turned to her mother. "Mommy, have you ever been to Paris with Grandma? Have you ever eaten a—what was it, Grandma?"

"*Croque monsieur*." Elizabeth made sure to emphasize the Gallic accent.

Sydney shook her head. "No, I have never been to Paris with Grandma, honey."

A steely tone crept into Elizabeth's voice as she studied the glowing tip of her cigarette. "Your mother wasn't interested in Paris, dear. Travel makes her anxious."

The temperature in the room suddenly seemed to lower a degree or two. "It wasn't the traveling that made me anxious, Mother."

"No?" Elizabeth asked.

"No," Sydney shot back.

Monica could feel the sharp tension between the two women, but she could tell that both were holding their tongues. Beth, thankfully, was oblivious to the strain. She merely picked up the music box, wound it up again, and put it down on the table, the pretty little notes of "Amazing Grace" resounding a musical truce over the taut room.

Chapter Four

As the meal went on, Elizabeth grew more garrulous, smoking cigarette after cigarette and downing successive glasses of iced tea. The stories she told—and she seemed to have a thousand of them—were becoming slightly unseemly, flirting with the downright indecent. Sydney was doing her best to control her temper, glancing at her daughter every so often to see if Beth had taken note of a bad word or a story too indelicate for a seven-year-old girl. For the most part, though, the little girl was content to let the grownups drone on while she wound up the music box over and over again.

Elizabeth's mind had turned to former lovers—and like her stories, she seemed to have had legions of those, too—and Monica was taken on a lengthy tour of the merits of various nationalities of men. American men, Monica discovered, ranked somewhere in the middle; Europeans—particularly the Italian and French—were, it seemed, in a constant battle for the number one slot.

"I think the last Italian man I dated was in Rome," Elizabeth exclaimed. "He was one of those new-wave movie directors. He was a beautiful man, but he could be mean, too." She drew in deeply on her cigarette. "Now what was his name? Wait a minute, I'll get it . . . I can remember his face"—she winked broadly at Monica—"as well as some other things."

"Oh, for goodness' sake, Mother," Sydney snapped, glancing toward Beth, hoping to remind her mother there was a child present without actually saying it. "I don't think anyone wants to hear this nonsense!"

Elizabeth fixed a gaze on her daughter. "Don't give me that holier-than-thou, pious little look of yours, Sydney." She grabbed another cigarette and lit it. "When was the last time you went out with a man, Sydney? It might do you some good, you know."

Monica did all she could to defuse the situation. "Ah, I . . . a nice, brisk walk in the morning always does me a lot of good," she said quickly.

Elizabeth exploded in laughter at Monica's comment and as she cackled she reached for the pitcher of iced tea, ready to refill her glass. But the gesture annoyed Sydney, who had been watching her mother with ever-increasing disgust as the dinner progressed. She grabbed the almost-empty pitcher from her mother and pulled it away.

"Hey," snapped Elizabeth. Her eyes were glassy and unfocused. "What do you think you're doing with that?"

Sydney stood firm. "You've had enough. That's what I'm doing. Mother, you have had enough iced tea for one night. Okay?"

"Enough? I don't think so . . ."

Sydney was still doing her best to control her anger. "Mother . . . can we please just have the cake and get this over with? Please? A piece of cake and we'll get out of here."

Elizabeth looked at her daughter as if she were speaking a foreign language. "Cake? What cake?"

"The birthday cake," said Sydney, glancing down at her daughter. Elizabeth had already ruined one cake, now it looked as if she had failed to provide the one she had promised for tonight.

Monica could not believe she had allowed herself to forget the birthday cake. There was only one way out now. She came to the rescue quickly.

"Of course," she said. "The cake. It's in the kitchen. I'll get it right away."

"That would be great," said Sydney, her voice tight and her words clipped and dry.

Monica vanished into the kitchen. She ran her fingers through her hair as she looked nervously around the room. Of course, there was no cake, she couldn't find anything that could even *pass* for a cake. There was certainly no time to bake. Monica knew that cake held a particular significance—a little girl's feelings were at stake. But most important, Monica was concerned about what this would do to the respect that Beth had for her grandmother.

There was only one thing Monica could do. She looked down at the empty kitchen counter, then closed her eyes and prayed . . . It took barely a moment and scarcely a thought from Monica before her prayer was answered. Even before she opened her eyes, she could sense the cake there on the counter, the gentle heat from the candles warming her face. Monica opened her eyes to see a perfect birthday cake. Thick white frosting decorated with a spray of pink and green roses made from spun sugar. "Happy Birthday, Beth" was spelled out in pink icing and seven white candles were artfully arranged around the name. The whole thing was set on a sterling silver cake platter.

Monica raised her eyes and smiled heavenward, expressing her heartfelt thanks. "Thank You," she whispered.

Things were not working out so well in the dining room. An angry silence hung in the room, mother and daughter studiously ignoring each other. Sydney did not know which was worse—that her mother had forgotten the cake or that a complete stranger, this Monica, had to be the one who remembered it.

Elizabeth put on an angry front, wondering out loud what the fuss was all about. It was just a *cake* after all; who really cared? At least, that's what Elizabeth pretended, but in the back of her mind she was feeling guilty and ashamed that she had completely forgotten about her own granddaughter's birthday cake.

Beth, completely unaware of the tension in the room, was happily winding up the ceramic

angel music box one more time. It seemed inno-
cent enough to the little girl—she had already
done it a dozen times that evening and no one
had objected to it.

But Elizabeth, who could feel Sydney's dis-
approval radiating across the table, allowed her
anger and guilt to get the better of her and she
struck out blindly.

"Oh, for goodness sake, Bethie," she snapped.
"Aren't you tired of that thing yet?" Elizabeth
lashed out and tried to grab the music box from
Beth's hand, a movement so quick and hard that
the little girl cried out in alarm and covered her
face, fearful that a blow would follow. She whim-
pered as she leaned behind her mother.

"Give it to me!" Elizabeth snapped. "I can't
stand it for one more minute!" She wrestled the
music box from the little girl's grasp. For a moment
Beth looked as if she might cry.

It took a second or two for Sydney to realize
what had happened. Then her features hardened.
She threw down her napkin and stood up quickly.

"That's it," she said, her eyes ablaze. "That is it!" She seized Beth by the wrist and pulled her to her feet. "Come on, Bethie, we're going."

Just then, Monica came back into the room carrying the gorgeous cake. Instantly she figured out what was going on. Her heart sank and she rushed to repair the situation.

"Oh, don't go," she said. She angled the cake toward them, showing them the beautiful frosting. "You must stay and have a piece of Beth's birthday cake. Look how lovely it is."

Sydney did her best to get her anger in check. None of the problems in that household were of Monica's making and she did not deserve to feel the sting of Sydney's rage.

"No, no," said Sydney firmly. "I'm sorry, Monica. This party is over. We'll be back tomorrow and have the cake. Please, Monica, can you save us some?"

"Of course," said Monica. "We'll wait until tomorrow to cut it. I'll put new candles on it."

"That's a great idea. Thank you." As Sydney

spoke, she gently pulled Beth toward the door. She could not get her daughter out of that house fast enough.

Elizabeth had not stirred from the table. She looked cooly at her daughter who was making a hasty retreat. "Sydney," she said sternly. "Beth wants some cake."

As much of a hurry as she was in to get out of there, Sydney had to stop. She turned and faced her mother down. "What she wants is a sober grandmother." Then she started toward the door again. "Come on, Beth, let's get out of here."

Monica rushed around from the table and caught up with Sydney and Beth as they put on their coats in the entrance hall of the old house. She put out a hand to stop Sydney long enough to talk to her.

"Sydney," she whispered. "I'm so sorry. I just didn't realize what was going on. I didn't know about your mother . . ."

"What?" Sydney snapped. "What do you mean?

Isn't that why her publisher sent you down here? To keep an eye on her?"

"No . . . ," said Monica, shaking her head. "No one there knows—" She glanced down at Beth, unsure if she should say anything in front of such a young child. "I didn't know she had a drinking problem."

Sydney's features hardened. "Drinking problem?" she said. She almost laughed. "My mother doesn't have a drinking problem, Monica. My mother is an alcoholic!" With that she pulled Beth out the front door and slammed it behind her.

Monica slowly made her way back to the dining room. Elizabeth was pouring herself yet another glass of "iced tea" (which was, in fact, a lethal mixture of vodka, tequila, light rum, and gin with a dash of cola to disguise it as a more benevolent drink). She took a sip of the brew and smiled crookedly at Monica, who had picked up the cake and was taking it back to the kitchen. She turned her back to her hostess.

"So," said Elizabeth. She lit a cigarette, sucked deeply, and then exhaled a great cloud of smoke. "Now you've met my daughter. Kind of a bore, don't you think?"

Monica did not answer. Her heart full of sorrow, she blew out the seven candles on the cake and wished that she had found some way to make the second attempt at Beth's birthday celebration a happier one.

Elizabeth sat at the dining table smoking and drinking, moodily staring into space, oblivious to Monica who had briskly set herself to clearing the wreckage of the dinner table. She scraped and stacked the plates and began washing them— she wasn't too sure of herself when it came to using a dishwasher. When she returned to the dining room, she found the iced tea pitcher empty, the ashtray full, and her hostess gone.

Monica walked through the silent house, the old floorboards creaking under her feet. She paused outside of Elizabeth's bedroom door and pushed it slightly ajar. Elizabeth was draped across the bed, one arm thrown over her eyes as if trying to protect them from a bright light though there was no more illumination in the room than the dull glow of a bedside lamp. Monica did her best to make Elizabeth comfortable, covering her with a blanket and turning out the light. Elizabeth was sleeping so heavily, so sodden by her endless glasses of iced tea, that she did not stir once. Monica tiptoed out of the room.

A few moments later she was back in Elizabeth's study, turning her attention to the stack of handwritten pages of the memoir.

. . . I screamed and complained and yelled so loud for so long that finally my editors gave in and assigned me to Saigon during the Vietnam War. I think they sent me hoping I would get killed. Well . . . maybe just scared to death. Or scared

enough to beg to come home the first time things got a little hot. The photographer they assigned to me was a daredevil kid from Boston, Brian Kelleher, and the two of us, a black woman from the South and a white kid from South Boston, went off to war. That was April 1964.

I wasn't the first woman to cover the war in Vietnam, but I was one of the first, and the guys down at the Foreign Press Club in Saigon were like journalists everywhere back then. Women might be able to cover women's issues, they might even be allowed to write the police blotter or even pieces of the metro section, but they had no business being war correspondents. We weren't tough enough, don't ya' know. Of course, that first night at the Press Club in Saigon, none of them were brazen enough to say so—no, they were much more subtle. As Brian and I sat at our table, the "guys" sent over round after round of complimentary cocktails. Well, that was okay—like I've said, I knew how to drink already—but our benefactors never sent the same drinks twice. A tray of martinis was followed by two glasses of scotch, then bourbon, then they switched to exotic mixed drinks like Rob Roys and Rusty Nails and Sidecars—the kinds of cocktails people drank back then, before the discovery of white wine. I knew what they were up to, of course, and I downed every one of those drinks, one after another. There was no way I was going to let them think that I couldn't hold my liquor. I was still standing long after most of them had passed out—Brian was asleep under the table by the fourth round. Eventually it was just me and an old warhorse from the UPI, a reporter who had been in Vietnam longer than any other. He opened two bottles of beer, handed one to me, threw his arm over my shoulder and breathed in my face—I can still smell it!—and he said, "Welcome to the war, kid . . . You're gonna do just fine!"

We clinked bottles and I downed mine without stopping. I felt like I had just been awarded the Medal of Honor. I was in; I was a member of the club and that meant something.

TOUGH LOVE

I spent my first full day in Vietnam with a hangover that almost killed me. Luckily, there was no news that day . . .

Chapter Five

*I*t was the day after the disastrous birthday dinner, and Elizabeth had managed to pull herself out of a massive hangover, largely by dint of sheer will, a succession of cups of hot, bitter coffee, and a lot of aspirin. When Sydney and Beth arrived that afternoon, it was plain that there had been an unspoken agreement between mother and daughter to paper over the unpleasantness of the night before. If Sydney and Elizabeth were going to unravel the tangled skein of problems they shared, then nothing was going to get done that day.

Beth finally got her birthday cake. Elizabeth, Sydney, and Beth were very impressed with what they took to be Monica's handiwork, but Monica refused to take the credit. "It was made by a friend of mine," she said. "A very dear friend."

They sang a rousing version of "Happy Birthday," Beth made her birthday wish before blowing out the candles, and Monica cut the cake.

Elizabeth took a bite and exclaimed in delight, "Angel food!"

Monica looked startled and paled a little. "I beg your pardon," she said.

"Angel food cake," Elizabeth exclaimed again. "This is my all-time favorite . . . so airy, so light. Tell your friend that I've never had a cake quite so good."

"I will," said Monica.

"It's awfully good," Sydney agreed. "Better than devil's food, any day."

The terms were completely foreign to Monica, but she found herself agreeing. "Oh yes," she concurred. "Much better than devil's food, anytime."

"I don't know," said Elizabeth. "I love angel food cake, but I had a devil's food cockaigne at Taillevant in Paris once that was just heavenly." She took another bite and smiled. "But this is better . . ."

"Yummy," Beth agreed. She giggled as Sydney attempted to make her sit still while she wiped a spot of frosting from Beth's chin.

There was no sign of yesterday's ubiquitous pitcher of iced tea, which Monica took to be a good sign.

After she finished dabbing at the frosting on Beth's smiling face, Sydney asked, "Mother, do you have any idea where my birth certificate might be?"

"It's in my files somewhere," said Elizabeth casually. "I know it's there. All we have to do is find it."

Monica started to clear the table and Elizabeth took her granddaughter by the hand and led her into the study. "Come on, Bethie," she said. "There's something I want to show you."

Parked on the cluttered desk in the study was Elizabeth Jessup's old manual typewriter, an Underwood that must have dated from the 1940s. On the far side of the room, Monica and Sydney sat on the floor going through Elizabeth's voluminous files, files that corresponded to Elizabeth's rather idiosyncratic system. But Elizabeth was focused completely on her little granddaughter.

"You have to learn to type, Beth," her grandmother informed her. "Even with computers you still need to know how to touch-type. And type fast . . ."

"We use computers at school," Beth proudly informed her.

"Computers are good," Elizabeth replied. "I never got the hang of them, but you learn to type on this old thing, and you'll be able to type on anything."

Elizabeth rolled a piece of paper into the old machine and put her granddaughter's tiny hands on the well-worn keys. Beth punched at the keys, her little fingers straining to work the old, stiff mechanism. She did manage to bang out a word or two.

"A little harder," said Elizabeth, standing over her. Beth punched at a few more keys, putting as much weight behind them as she could. "That's good," said Elizabeth. "But you have to type really fast . . . Now, see, this is the first rule of journalism, darling. You must learn to type faster than you think . . . That way you're sure you'll never miss a story."

Beth looked a little doubtful about this. "I don't know, Grandma. I think pretty fast."

Elizabeth laughed. "Yes, you certainly do think fast," she said. "And you are going to make a wonderful reporter one day."

As Beth did her best to work the old type-writer—the dogged determination on her face a mirror of her grandmother's—Sydney called from across the room, "You know I didn't come here to clean out your files, Mother."

Both she and Monica were knee-deep in piles

of yellowing paper, bulging reporter's note-books, old address books, canceled passports, copies of wire service stories that were decades old. The clutter that accumulates throughout a very busy career.

"Good," grumbled Elizabeth. "I don't want my files cleaned out. If I find one piece of paper missing—"

"How would you be able to tell?" Sydney asked. There seemed to be no rhyme or reason to the organization of the mounds of papers.

"I'll be able to tell," Elizabeth replied. "You can bet on it, Sydney. I will notice."

"Well, then, can you just give me an idea of the general vicinity of my birth certificate?"

Elizabeth sounded slightly annoyed. "Sydney, *why* on earth do you need your birth certificate? The only thing you'd need it for is a new passport and I know you don't need one of those . . . Oh, and I guess you need one for a marriage license too. Also unlikely. Am I right?"

Monica looked from mother to daughter. First

came the bickering, tensions rose, and then Elizabeth went for the bottle. She hoped that this argument did not escalate and follow the now-familiar pattern.

"There is another reason," said Sydney, keeping her cool. "I need it because I got promoted at the bank and they're running a new security check system."

Elizabeth backed down too. She scratched her head and thought for a moment. "Okay . . . Sydney's birth certificate . . ." She closed her eyes as if trying to conjure up an image of the document. "Birth certificate . . . Um, check the file under *M*."

"*M*?" said Sydney. "Why *M*?"

"You were born during the Six-Day War—a major event in the Middle East," Elizabeth said, as if her system made perfect sense. "So check *M* for Middle East."

Sydney shot Monica a "you see what I'm up against" look and pulled a tattered folder from a box. It was marked with a big black *M*. Sydney slapped it open and flipped through a few pages and found her birth certificate.

"Bingo," said Sydney. "Got it."

"See," said Monica. "Her system works for her. Who says any other way of filing would be better?"

"I suppose so . . ." Sydney was caught up in the contents of the *M* folder, glancing through the various fascinating documents: Elizabeth's Israeli Defense Force security clearance card, a sheaf of articles that recorded the tensions leading up to the Six-Day War—and then there was a gap from Sydney's birth through the end of the war.

Elizabeth may have missed the war, but everyone in the world of journalism knew that at one time she had been a major player on the international scene. Sydney held up a letter and showed it to Monica. "Wow," she said. "Take a look at this."

"'Dear Liz . . . ,'" Sydney read. "It's from Moshe Dayan—" Dayan had been the dashing Israeli general who masterminded and directed

the stunning success of Israel over her many enemies back in 1967.

Sydney scanned down the letter quickly, then
laughed. "He apologizes for not being able to
prolong the Six-Day War to accommodate her,
but he congratulates her on having a daughter."

"That's you," said Monica.

Sydney nodded and looked over at her mother.
Elizabeth was still tutoring Beth on the finer
points of being a professional journalist. She was
completely unaware of the warm, loving look in
her daughter's dark eyes.

"She was quite a woman," Sydney said softly.

Monica nodded. "She's still someone to be
proud of," she said. "She must have been an
exciting person to have as a mother."

"On those rare occasions when Mother was
actually around," said Sydney with a hint of regret.
"I seem to remember that she traveled about
three hundred and sixty-three days a year. But,
sometimes she even made it home for Christmas,
you know."

"You never traveled with her?" Monica asked. The night before, Elizabeth had said that travel made her daughter "anxious." Monica wondered exactly what she meant.

Sydney nodded. "Oh, yeah, sure . . . I did, several times. When I was much younger."

"That must have been quite an experience. Did you enjoy it?" Monica asked.

"Sometimes . . ." Sydney took a deep breath. "I went with her to New York, and Washington a couple of times. And believe it or not, I went to Russia once too."

"Washington and Russia? What a study in contrasts that must have been."

Sydney nodded and laughed quietly. "You can say that again. On the whole, I think I prefer Washington."

"Tell me about it," Monica asked.

Sydney's face seemed to glow for a moment. "It was magical," she said. ". . . like a dream. Everywhere we went people knew her. Important people—politicians, movie stars, people I used to see on TV. Even people on the street recognized her because she used to be on those Sunday morning opinion shows. We went to political conventions; I met Coretta Scott King, Jackie Kennedy . . . We'd stay at these wonderful hotels and I'd sneak down to the ballrooms at night and hide, watching my mother in the middle of a crowd. They were listening to her, hanging on her every word." Sydney closed her eyes, savoring the memory.

"I can still see her standing there, dressed to the nines, a champagne glass in her hand, holding court. Telling people how things really were. She would go out in the streets, into the slums, and she'd bring back the real news. She was at home in the ghettos as much as she was in the glittering halls." Sydney opened her eyes and smiled, shaking her head slowly. "But she always had that champagne glass in her hand." She sighed. "If only things had turned out differently. If only she were still that woman, the one from so long ago."

Monica shook her head. "She still is, Sydney. It's just that your mother is hurting, deep down inside."

Sydney shrugged. "It's so hard to accept; I find it hard to believe that a woman so strong in other ways can't find it in herself to control something so destructive."

"It's not that easy," said Monica. "You have to understand that, Sydney."

Sydney gave Monica a knowing look. "Believe me, I do understand." She turned back to the pile of papers, closing up the *M* file and putting it back into the old brown file box. That just left the more recent scatter of mail and newspapers that littered the top of the coffee table. Sydney's eyes fell on an invitation card written in ornate copperplate script and embossed with the seal of the city. She picked it up and read it.

"Mother," Sydney asked. "What is this?" She held up the card and waved it.

"What is what, dear?" Elizabeth sounded distracted as she continued to help her granddaughter with the old typewriter. She scarcely bothered to glance at her daughter.

"This is an invitation to the mayor's Centennial Kickoff," said Sydney.

"Yes, so?"

"It says you are one of the speakers," Sydney continued. "You speak right after the mayor."

"Oh . . . I'll think of something to say," said Elizabeth, sounding very high-handed. "I don't want to talk about it right now. It's not until the fifteenth anyway. It's a long way off."

Sydney gaped at her mother for a moment. "Mother, this *is* the fifteenth."

The news did nothing to shake Elizabeth. She hardly looked up from the task at hand. "Well, then," she said. "I guess I'm not going."

"Oh," said Monica, "but they're expecting you. You're one of the guests of honor."

Elizabeth shook her head. "No . . . They're expecting a beautiful, intrepid, roving foreign correspondent and . . . let's face it, I am not as roving as I used to be."

To Monica the solution seemed simple. "Well, maybe it's time you started again."

The city had put on a very nice spread for the inauguration of the centennial year. A red, white, and blue marquee had been erected on the lawn of City Hall, and under it sat the mayor and a host of city officials and dignitaries. Sydney, Beth, and Monica sat at the extreme left of the row of luminaries. Their seats had been added at the last minute, as there had been no confirmation from Elizabeth. When she arrived with three guests in tow, arrangements were hastily made.

On her way to her seat Elizabeth had discovered the bar the city had set up in the park for the celebration that would follow the ceremony. The bartender was not supposed to give out any drinks until the formalities were over, but Elizabeth turned on the charm and cajoled the man into giving her a glass of white wine, then another, then a third, while she listened to initial speakers. She managed to get a fourth glass out of the bartender, telling him that she was on after the mayor and she needed to steady her nerves. The bartender, who was no stranger to drunks, was sure that Elizabeth was stone-cold sober. Besides, she looked fabulous. She was dressed in black heels, a tight-fitting black skirt, and a white blazer of a vaguely military cut, an effect emphasized by navy blue flashes adorned with gold thread. She wore very dark sunglasses that made her look sophisticated and younger than her years.

The bartender handed over the final glass without a second thought. Elizabeth smiled and winked.

"Thanks, honey . . ." She took a gulp and turned her attention to the remarks of the mayor.

The mayor had taken the audience through the first hundred years of the history of the city—her founding fathers, her distinguished citizens past and present.

"And so," said the mayor, "on this, the one-hundredth anniversary of our city, it is only fitting that the best of the best be placed in our time capsule to represent us for eternity . . . which brings me to Elizabeth Jessup. Elizabeth's distinguished career as a journalist of international reputation is second to none. And her many prestigious awards are too numerous to mention."

Elizabeth laughed to herself, took a sip of wine and muttered: "Oh, go on. Mention them! I worked too hard for those baubles to go and forget about 'em now."

As if he had heard her, the mayor obliged. "However, we do have to mention that Elizabeth Jessup has won the Foreign Press Medal and, of course, the most coveted award in all of American journalism—the Pulitzer prize. She has been courageous in the face of war and disaster and—even politics." There was polite laughter from the audience. "She has brought honor to herself and credit to her hometown. Ladies and gentlemen . . . please welcome the legendary Ms. Elizabeth Jessup."

Elizabeth threw away her cigarette, put down her glass, and languidly took off her sunglasses, strolling toward the podium with studied nonchalance. As she passed Monica and Sydney she whispered: "Did you hear that? Legendary."

She stood at the lectern for a moment waiting for the applause to die down. When it was quiet enough for her to speak she leaned into the microphone.

"Thank you, thank you, I can't tell you what a thrill it is to be here with you today . . . The reason I can't tell you is because I forgot to write my speech . . ." She got too close to the mikes and a wave of feedback rang through the air, the whine mixing with the laughter from the audience.

"But," she continued, "I am touched that you are including me in your time capsule . . . or rather, my writings . . . I can't imagine I'd be comfortable inside that thing . . ."

There was a little more laughter, but it was weak and forced. Something was not quite right about Elizabeth's speech. While not slurred exactly, her words were not those of an eloquent, prizewinning journalist.

"But it would be a great honor to be interred with . . ." Elizabeth half-turned toward the mayor. "What did you say was in there, Mister Mayor? A pound of wheat, a picture of our new library . . ." Elizabeth gave a shrug, a dismissive gesture. "Wow . . . That ought to set their hair on fire in a hundred years." The audience laughed again, but people were getting uncomfortable.

Then the alcohol kicked in and really loosened Elizabeth's tongue. "How 'bout a nude picture of me instead?" There were gasps from the audience but Elizabeth was oblivious to them. "Or how 'bout a picture of all of us? Right now. That would do it, wouldn't it?" Elizabeth cackled and shook her head. "'Those guys a hundred years ago sure knew how to make history' they'll say . . ." Then she paused again, and she seemed to be churning up a memory. "That reminds me. I saw the mayor naked once . . ."

Every eye was on the mayor now and he shifted uncomfortably in his seat.

Elizabeth was oblivious to the mayor's discomfort and the general uneasiness of the audience. She plowed on. "Yup. Saw him naked. He dived right into the pool at the country club and his shorts fell off." Elizabeth giggled. "Talk about a news flash."

Sydney was on her feet now, trying to pull her mother away from the podium. "Mom, that's enough."

A slice of speech she had given once popped into Elizabeth's drink-addled brain. "Struggled against great and significant obstacles all the time . . ."

Sydney managed to get ahold of one of the microphones. "I'm . . . I'm sorry," she said. "She's on antibiotics and she really shouldn't be drinking right now." She tried to pull her mother away from the podium, but Elizabeth fought back.

"I'm not finished yet," Elizabeth yelled.

"Mother, let's go." Sydney was using all her strength to get her mother off the stage.

"You never like to see me in the spotlight, do you, Sydney?" Elizabeth demanded.

As she was yanked offstage, the mayor reclaimed the podium. "Elizabeth Jessup, ladies and gentlemen."

He clapped his hands, trying to get some kind of halfhearted applause going. People clapped, but not for long. The crowd watched Elizabeth being led away, a sad shell of her former self.

Monica helped Sydney steer her mother well away from the ceremony, but it was no easy task to get her out of the park. First, Elizabeth thought she deserved to go to the party following the speeches, then she thought she would drive herself home.

"Let me drive you, please, Mother?" Sydney pleaded. "It'll only take a minute. Or you can come to our house. Take a little nap."

"That means sleep one off," Elizabeth snapped. She was hopping mad at the treatment she had received at the hands of her daughter. "I'm going home." She started away, then stopped and turned on Sydney, as if she had just remembered something. "And how dare you? How dare you tell people I'm taking antibiotics . . . How dare you mention my drinking habits in public?" She turned away again. "Now where is that bathroom?" She stumbled a few steps. "There's got to be a bathroom around here someplace . . ."

Elizabeth recovered her balance and, holding her head high, walked away with the elaborate care and exaggerated dignity of the drunk. Sydney tried again to stop her. "Mother . . . Mother, please don't . . ."

But Elizabeth brushed her off and refused to even look at her. "I don't need you to help me go to the bathroom," she said. "So, Sydney, back off."

Sydney watched her go and sighed, her eyes brimming with tears. She was aware of Monica standing behind her and she could feel her sympathetic gaze on her back. Sydney spoke to her without turning around.

"Do you have any idea what it is like to watch your own mother self-destruct?" She was silent for a long, long time, sinking down on a park bench, closing her eyes and shaking her head. Monica sat down next to her, ready to help.

"I love her," Sydney said after a long while. "She's . . . she's my mother, but I have given up."

"Oh, no," said Monica. She knew how corrosive despair could be. It either brought you to your knees, to that vulnerable place where you find the mercy of God or it took you to the door of destruction. She put her hands on Sydney's shoulders. "You must never give up, Sydney. That is something you can never do, for your mother, for yourself, and for Beth."

Sydney did her best to pull herself together, wiping the tears from her eyes. "You know what the really hard thing is? It's . . . it's that . . . I know what I have to do. I know what I need to do. I know what it's going to take . . . It's just that I can't do it alone . . ."

A smile stole over Monica's face and with it came a look of gentle but firm determination. There was a good heart in this woman and Monica was determined to find it and reclaim it for her family. "Well, then," she said resolutely. "I'll help you. That's what I'm here for, after all . . . Now, let's get your mother home."

Chapter Six

*M*onica and Sydney succeeded in getting Elizabeth back to her house with little difficulty. Elizabeth had sat sullenly in the car, like a bad-tempered child who thought herself unfairly rebuked. From time to time she opened her mouth to defend her actions and her words at the reception, but spoke very little before realizing that no one was interested in what she had to say. Rather, Elizabeth contented herself with muttering under her breath. Monica caught just a little of what she said: "Small people. You're all small people . . ."

When they arrived at the house, Elizabeth kicked off her high heels, opened the car door, and swept up the short driveway without so much as a glance behind her. Sydney watched her as she went, shook her head and turned to Monica.

"I'll come in," she said.

"No," said Monica. "That's really not necessary. It's no trouble."

"She's my mother," said Sydney.

"I understand that," Monica replied. "But if she's going to say something hurtful let her say it to me. And if you'd want to say something hurtful to her," Monica shrugged, "you won't be there to say it."

The young woman looked at Monica for a long moment. "It's not your fight."

"It's not yours either," Monica returned. She glanced up the path toward Elizabeth's retreating back. "It's hers . . ."

By the time Monica walked in, Elizabeth had already poured herself a tall glass of tea and retired to her bedroom. It was only late afternoon, but she managed to give the distinct impression that she would not be seen again that day.

At six o'clock Monica knocked on her door. It took a couple of tries, but eventually there was a groggy grunt from the other side of the bedroom door.

"Elizabeth?" Monica called through the partition.

"What?"

"It's six o'clock. Would you like something to eat? Can I make you a little supper?"

There was a long silence from inside the bedroom. For a moment Monica was afraid that Elizabeth had dozed off. She rapped on the door again.

"Elizabeth?"

"Not hungry. Need sleep. Go away . . ."

Monica sighed and returned to her duties in the study, working at the typewriter on Elizabeth's memoirs.

The busiest time of my life was during the middle to late seventies. I seemed to live on airplanes—not only did I know the names of flight attendants on a half dozen airlines, I knew the names of their kids and their husbands as well. It was about this time I sort of forgot the names of mine . . . Well, I never forgot my daughter, of course, but my husband and I had drifted apart. He wanted a home life—and I wanted a life.

My daughter, Sydney was, of course, completely on my side. She traveled with me as much as possible—we had a rule in my family: no kids allowed in a war zone! To the chagrin of her schoolteachers, I was always yanking Sydney out of school and taking her with me to Washington, New York, London. It seemed to me that a young girl got a lot more of an education by actually going to Buckingham Palace or the United Nations than by simply hearing about them from some bore of a teacher in a drab middle school. As I used to tell her, you'll have plenty of time for a dull life. I know she agreed then and I'm sure she agrees now

that she's a mother—the mother of my beautiful
granddaughter.

Monica looked up from the typewriter and
sifted through her thoughts of this brilliant and
complex woman's life. She wondered if Elizabeth
had managed to repeat these ideas to herself until
she actually believed them or if she was just telling
things the way she had hoped they had been.
Either way, Monica had the feeling she had con-
structed a fantasy of the past—her own, her husband's, and her daughter's.

Monica read on.

But not even Sydney could keep up with me
back then. In my assignment diary for 1975, I see
that the beginning of the year had me in Washington
covering the sentencing of four Watergate figures:
John Mitchell, H. R. Haldeman, John Erlichman,
and Robert Mardian. You might recognize three
of those names—but I bet I'm the only one around
here who remembers that Bob Mardian had his

conviction overturned and all charges against him dropped.

From Washington I was thrown into the most harrowing story of my entire professional life. Earlier in the year, the Khmer Rouge began its murderous rampage in Cambodia and it had become my story. Getting into the country was hard. I sat on the Vietnamese-Cambodian border for almost a week, screaming and yelling, whispering and cajoling, and finally paid a big fat bribe to get across the frontier. I got into Phnom Penh feeling like I was on the verge of the story of a lifetime, a second Pulitzer for sure. But it did not take me long to realize that I would be lucky if I got out of there with my life.

From there Monica read Elizabeth's eyewitness account of the bloodstained rampage of the Communist guerrillas who had taken over the troubled land of Cambodia. No matter how dangerous the moment, no matter how gory the scenes Elizabeth personally witnessed, she had managed to commit every event, every moment to memory or paper. Monica marveled at the strength of this woman. She had not only the courage to go through the Khmer Rouge massacres in real life, but to unflinchingly call up those terrible memories once again to put them down in her memoirs.

I was out of Cambodia before I knew it—and believe me I was glad to get out of there. But I went from one awful situation to another. After more than twenty-five years of war, with more than one million Vietnamese and 56,000 Americans dead, South Vietnam was being overrun by the forces of North Vietnam and the Vietcong. I was being sent back to Vietnam to cover the end of my first war. Saigon was falling . . . From a journalistic point of view, it was a terrific story. It had everything—war, death, tragedy, injustice, panic— you name it, it had it . . . the kind of carrion that journalists had no trouble making a meal of. I hooked up with my old pal Brian. His pictures and my words told the horrific story. The funny thing is that on the day Saigon actually fell, the day that famous helicopter took off from the roof of the U.S. Embassy, all I could think of was the fact that my little Sydney was graduating from second grade. That very day.

On April 30, 1975, I was a witness to history. But what I really wanted to witness was my little girl in a cap and gown made out of construction paper, up there on the stage reciting the Pledge of Allegiance. I wanted to see that smile, that smile with the gaps and the baby teeth . . . I told Brian about Sydney as we watched the last chopper lift off from the embassy roof. He shot a few frames, said something obscene with a mischievous smile, and suggested we go and get a drink before the Commies banned liquor forever here in the new worker's paradise. I thought he had a point, so that's what we did. There was a lot of news the next day and I covered it through a colossal hangover.

The rest of the year was just as crazy as the beginning. On my way home from the Pacific, the *paper decided that I was in the perfect position to cover the latest breaking story—the independence of the Island of Papua New Guinea . . . Don't get me wrong. I was thrilled for New Guinea, but I wanted to get home. I missed Sydney so much. I filed my story, and attended a nice party afterward. There was no news the next day, which was a good thing, if you know what I mean . . .*

Elizabeth landed in San Francisco the day the FBI finally caught up with Patty Hearst, who had been kidnapped the year before by the Symbionese Liberation Army. Much against her will Elizabeth was sent out to cover that story.

Still on the West Coast, a long way from home, she was assigned to the oddest story of her career. Elizabeth was sent to cover the Muhammad Ali versus Joe Frazier heavyweight bout, the famous "Thrilla in Manila." Ali knocked out Frazier in the fourteenth round, which touched off a party that lasted quite a while. "*They drink some pretty strange stuff in the Philippines,*" she explained, *"but once the party was over, thank God I had enough brain cells left to remember to get Sydney autographed pictures of Ali and Frazier. And this time I made it all the way home . . ."*

Monica wasn't quite sure what she should make of all this. She had the sense that on the one hand Elizabeth was still proud of her drinking, still believing that it was some sort of badge of honor, a talisman that proved she had been accepted by the old boys' club—that she could cover a war, a prizefight, and a massacre and still drink the best man under the table. And yet, Monica also sensed that Elizabeth felt genuinely bad about the way she had behaved. She was ashamed of the way she had neglected her daughter, and contrite in the face of her own ambition.

But I wasn't home for long. By November I was back in Europe to cover the death of the last totalitarian leader in Western Europe, General Francisco Franco of Spain. The story goes that as Franco lay on his deathbed in his palace he heard the sound of a large crowd gathering in the square outside his window. He summoned a servant and asked what was going on. "Your people, Generalissimo, are assembling to say good-bye." "Really," Franco replied, "where are they all going?"

The truth of it was, I didn't see a lot of tears shed for the old fascist. Of course, I didn't stay around long after he died. Lebanon had just erupted in a bloody civil upheaval and I was on my way to cover what I considered to be my second war. I don't count the events I witnessed in Cambodia—that wasn't war, that was murder, pure and simple.

And so it went. Monica read page after page. There did not seem to be an event that decade that Elizabeth had not reported in some way or another. Sometimes she was dispatched to cover old ground—her paper appeared to have staked out anything in the Middle or Far East for her, and sometimes she just happened to be in the right place at the right time when news was breaking.

It went on like this year after year. It was an exciting life and I saw some amazing things, but at the same time, as a mother, my heart was broken. When I think back on the number of little things I didn't get to see my little girl do—those small anniversaries of childhood—it still brings tears to my eyes. One year, in 1978, I thought I had it all worked out. I got home the week before Christmas and managed to do all the shopping for presents, pulled together the ingredients for Christmas dinner, and got everything wrapped. Sydney, my mother, and I decorated the tree on Christmas Eve and, once Sydney went to bed, I sat up sipping eggnog and putting together that most complicated of children's toys: a bicycle. (Let me just note here that eggnog is not the best thing to be drinking when you are dealing with fine print, hard steel, and complicated instructions.) Anyway, I built it and fell into bed only to be awakened an hour or two later. Sydney was up and wanted to open her presents. Fair enough. Mother and I got up with her and sat in the living room as my beautiful little girl opened her presents. She was just ripping the paper off the first one when the phone rang.

We all froze and I can still see the look on Sydney's face, that pleading look, begging me not to answer the phone . . . Well, I answered the phone. It was, of course, the foreign desk in New York. Vietnam had chosen Christmas morning to invade Cambodia. With the sound of Sydney sobbing fresh in my ears, I set off for my third war . . .

Late the next afternoon, Elizabeth emerged from her bedroom acting as though nothing had happened. She showed no indication that getting up so late was due to anything besides being a little more tired than usual. She made a cup of coffee and plunked herself down in the living room to read the newspaper. Monica had already read it and, before finding the story on the Centennial celebration, she had feared the worst.

But Elizabeth had retired to a small enough town that the newspaper would not make fun of its only Pulitzer prize-winner. Everyone would know soon enough that the town's most famous daughter had been falling-down drunk at a municipal affair without having to read about it in the paper. The only person who seemed not to have realized the way news spread in a little town was Elizabeth herself. She seemed rather pleased with the way her performance had been reviewed, and if she thought she had dodged the bullet of public humiliation, she gave no sign of it.

With some pride, she read the account of the celebration aloud to Monica. "'The mayor's comments were followed by the raucous and humorous reflections of a Pulitzer prize-winning journalist,'" Elizabeth read out loud. "Did you hear that? 'Raucous,'" she repeated. "See. They loved me . . . don't know what Sydney was making such a fuss over yesterday." She looked at the paper, rereading the brief column. "You know, I'm surprised they can spell *raucous*."

If it was a joke, Monica refused to be drawn into it. "I'm surprised that you find a word like *raucous* to be a compliment," she said. "I was always given to believe that raucous behavior was not something you strove for."

Elizabeth grunted. "Huh. Sounds like someone took a hissy pill first thing this morning."

Before Monica could reply, the doorbell chimed. "I'll get that," she said, rising from her place on the sofa.

"Don't bother," said Elizabeth, turning back to the newspaper. "It's probably no one important."

Monica knew exactly who it was and she continued on her way to the front door. Elizabeth looked up. "What did I say, Monica? I said, don't get that."

Monica turned, her eyes full of sadness. She

had come to like Elizabeth. Her wisdom in writing and genuine concern for others were often hidden by a false front of imperiousness and her tendency to be overbearing—and Monica now felt sorry for the older woman. A bombshell was about to burst over her and she didn't have the slightest idea what was coming.

"I'm sorry, Elizabeth," said Monica deliberately. "But this time I have to."

Elizabeth shrugged and went back to her newspaper. Whatever was bothering Monica was *not* bothering her. Moments later Sydney, Beth, and Monica filed into the room. A heavy silence filled the room. Beth looked up at her mother with fear in her eyes and clutched her soft toy rabbit tightly to her chest.

Elizabeth was puzzled by the grave expressions. "Is there something wrong?" she asked.

Sydney took a deep breath. The blood pulsed in her veins and her tongue felt thick. It was hard to talk to one's mother like this, to tell the disturbing truth to a tormented parent. It was a change of roles—the child had become the nurturing and caring parent, the parent the stubborn and unruly child.

"Mother . . . ," Sydney began. "We're here today because . . . because we love you."

Elizabeth was no fool. She knew that her daughter and granddaughter had come to say much more than that. Things that she probably did not want to hear.

"Good," she said with a thin smile. "Same here. I love you too." She looked back to her paper. "Now, if you'll excuse me . . . I don't mean to be rude, but I do have quite a bit of work to do. I'll see you later, okay, Sydney? Bethie?"

"No, Mother," said Sydney. "This is something that cannot wait until later." She sat down on the sofa next to her mother and allowed Beth to sit on her lap. "We're concerned about you," she said, "and we don't know any other way to let you know."

"And just what are you concerned about?"

Elizabeth asked, her voice sharp and angry. "If I were you, Sydney, I'd be more concerned about my own life."

But this was one time Sydney was determined not to be pushed around.

"We are concerned about you and your drinking," said Sydney firmly. "And something has to be done about it. Here and now. You can't ignore it any longer—and neither can we." Sydney felt out of breath; it had taken real exertion to get the words out of her mouth.

Elizabeth said nothing, but leaned to her side on the sofa, resting her head on her hand, looking at her daughter firmly, thinking she must have suddenly taken leave of her senses. Then the angle of her gaze shifted and her eyes widened. A complete stranger, a woman in her late thirties or early forties, had just walked into the living room of her house.

"Now, just who are you?" Elizabeth demanded. "What is this all about?"

"This is Anita," said Sydney as calmly as she

could. "She is a counselor at the New Hope Center. She is willing to help us help you."

Anita was a veteran of dozens of family interventions with alcoholics and drug addicts. She never knew what kind of response she would receive, but she was always ready for anything. Today she had brought a stack of papers with her, along with what appeared to be a couple of Beth's childlike drawings and paintings.

"Hello, Elizabeth," she said confidently. "I have spoken with your family and they have expressed to me their love for you. It is a deep and genuine love."

Elizabeth was staring at Anita as if she were speaking a foreign language.

Anita continued despite Elizabeth's disbelieving silence. "But they also feel that your drinking is getting in the way of your relationship with them. They agree that unless you get some help for your problem, you can no longer be part of their lives. They've written you letters about their feelings and how your drinking has affected them." She offered the papers in her hand. "Would you like to see them now?"

In a very small voice Beth said, "I drew mine with pictures."

More than anything Anita said, it was Beth's words that struck Elizabeth the most. They had even succeeded in turning her own granddaughter against her. Elizabeth felt the anger beginning to burn deep in the core of her being.

"Elizabeth," Anita quietly continued, "after you read their letters, Sydney and I have arranged to take you to the New Hope Center where you can begin our alcohol rehabilitation program."

Without moving a muscle, Elizabeth looked at her daughter, her eyes cold and hard. She spoke slowly and very clearly.

"Sydney, this is the single most asinine thing you've ever done in your entire life," she said.

"Mother," Sydney replied. "Please try to understand. We want to help you. Please listen to what we are telling you."

"Help me?" said Elizabeth, her voice still low,

but building in intensity. "You are trying to control me and I won't have it. Do you hear me? I won't! Now what I do in the privacy of my own home is none of your business."

"That's just the point, Elizabeth," said Anita. "It's not just happening in the privacy of your home any more. Your problems are hurting everyone who loves you."

But Elizabeth had gone beyond reason now and was beginning to shout. "And to let this stranger use my granddaughter to get back at me for a problem that you have had with me ever since you could talk," she pointed an accusatory finger at Sydney. "That is reprehensible. I never thought I would see you stoop so low!"

"Mother," Sydney argued back, "your drinking is hurting her too. But you just don't see it."

Elizabeth's voice had dropped to a low whisper and she turned her back on all of them. "Get out of my house," she said. Her voice may have been low, but it was shot through with a deep, blazing rage.

Anita tried one last time to make Elizabeth understand. "Do you realize, Elizabeth, that your family will not have any contact with you until you are ready to admit to yourself that there is a problem and that you are ready to do something about it?"

Elizabeth whirled around and shouted at the top of her voice: *"I said, get out of my house!"*

The intensity of her rage was frightening. Sydney was close to tears and Beth was so frightened she buried her head in her mother's skirt and began to tremble. Only Anita stood confident and firm. She had seen worse in her days as a counselor, greater anger, louder roars—even physical violence. Monica stepped in to try to calm Elizabeth down. She made one last attempt to get her to see reason. "Elizabeth, please . . . You've got to—"

But Elizabeth was so caught up in the searing frenzy of anger that she would not listen to Monica or anyone else. "Get out!" she screamed, her voice high and piercing. "Get out all of you!

And don't you ever come back." She pointed a finger at Monica like a rifle bullet. "You too. Get out!! Get *out of my house!*"

Sydney gathered up Beth, and mother and child fled for the door. Even Monica, scared by the outburst, retreated against Elizabeth's overpowering anger. Anita held her ground long enough to make her professional statement. She pulled a business card from her purse and thrust it into Elizabeth's hand. In the confusion Elizabeth took it, not quite aware of what it was.

"I'm available at this number twenty-four hours a day," Anita said compassionately. "Whenever you're ready, call me. We can put all of this behind us. We can start again . . ."

But Elizabeth was still firmly in the clutches of her rage. "Out," she screamed. "Out! Out! Out! *Out* . . . !"

After they left, the house seemed very silent, but redolent somehow, with the echoes of Elizabeth's angry screams. She paced the living room, agitation on her like electricity. She was still angry, humiliated, and furious—enraged that she, Elizabeth Jessup, prizewinning journalist, a woman so well-known she could pick up the phone and get *presidents* to take her call, had been so mortified and embarrassed by her family. She felt Anita's card in her hand and tore it into a dozen pieces, throwing the confetti into the fireplace. Elizabeth stopped cold at the mantelpiece and looked at the pictures there, realizing that the thing that bothered her most was that she had frightened her granddaughter—her pride and joy and namesake—and had lessened herself in those young, trusting eyes.

Tears flowed easily when she admitted that to herself—and the great Elizabeth Jessup, the *legendary* Elizabeth Jessup, decided that what she really needed was a good stiff drink.

Chapter Seven

*I*t was not easy for Monica to make herself go back to Elizabeth's house the next morning. The vehemence and fury of the older woman's anger seemed to still hang in the air and Monica could still hear Elizabeth's outraged voice in her ears. She stepped gingerly into the house, peering around the door, hoping to catch a glimpse of Elizabeth so she could announce herself rather than barge into the house without an invitation.

"Hello?" she called out. "Is there anyone here?" She could barely see into the darkened house. "Elizabeth . . . Are you in there? It's me, Monica."

Monica took a tentative step into the house. It was silent and still and had a shut-in, airless quality. There was a heavy smell of stale cigarette smoke. She took another step inside. "Elizabeth . . . ?"

Elizabeth did not answer. Monica walked into the house and stopped. At her feet were the two letters that Sydney and Beth had written to explain their feelings toward Elizabeth and her drinking problem. She knelt down and picked up the letters. Sydney's was written out in a neat script that could have been a perfect facsimile of her mother's own handwriting. Monica could not help but read a few lines:

. . . those birthdays and Christmases. I understood you could not be there. I was proud of you and your job. Back in 1978—what was I, nine? Ten? I knew you had to leave. You had no reason to hate yourself or to resent me. That was our life back then and I accepted it. Today, Mother, it's a different story. Your drinking is going to kill you. But before it kills you it's going to kill our family . . .

Monica recognized the truth in the words and she knew that they came directly from Sydney's heart. She knew that Sydney was forcing herself and her mother to face the truth no matter how harsh that truth might be. It simply had to be done.

Beth's crumpled paper was even more heart-wrenching. The little girl had drawn a series of pictures in crayon, each alive with the straight-forward honesty of a child and with exceptional clarity of purpose no matter how crudely executed. One bright drawing, a riot of orange and purple, showed a woman stretched out on a couch fast asleep as a little girl valiantly tried to awaken her. A caption read, "Grandma won't wake up and play." Another showed the three Jessup women gathered around the dinner table. A large, half-empty pitcher was clearly labeled "iced tea" and the white tube in Elizabeth's hand was marked "cigarette" followed by a bracketed word, *bad*. An arrow pointed to Sydney and she was marked "Mommy." Mommy did not look happy. Neither did the figure of the little girl, marked "Me." The next picture depicted the scene that occurred a few days earlier when Elizabeth knocked the birthday cake from the arms of the waiter at the restaurant. The drawing indicated that the little girl knew that something bad had happened, something worse than the dropping of a birthday cake.

The last picture was the most disturbing. As best as the little girl could manage, Beth had tried to render an argument between Elizabeth and Sydney. As Monica studied the picture, she could feel Beth reaching to the limits of her skills to translate the anger in those two adult faces into the strokes of a crayon. Beth herself was a very small figure crouched in a far corner with blue dots streaming from her wide eyes, signifying uncomprehending tears.

"Oh, Beth," Monica whispered as tears welled in her own eyes. "You poor dear. You poor thing." She folded the two pieces of paper and walked a little farther into the house. "Elizabeth? It's me, Monica. Are you here? Are you okay?"

Elizabeth was sprawled on the living room sofa, still dressed in the clothes she had been wearing the night before. On the coffee table next to her were an empty liter bottle of bourbon and an ashtray filled to overflowing.

"Oh no, Elizabeth," said Monica. She could see that she wasn't so much sleeping as she was in a stupor. "How could you do this to yourself?"

Shaking her head, Monica made her way to Elizabeth's cluttered kitchen. Coffee, she knew, was something that people craved when they woke up in the morning and she knew it was given to drunks to try to sober them up. Monica was about to make her very first cup of what Tess called "Joe."

"I don't think you want to give her that," Tess said. She was standing in a corner of the kitchen, leaning on the table watching Monica's hapless efforts at putting the coffeepot together. "Coffee doesn't sober you up," she continued. "It just makes you wide awake. And your friend in there is not going to want to feel wide awake.

What she will want is something to stop the throbbing headache that's going to wake her up and something to make her feel a little more human again. Alcohol dehydrates. She's going to be thirsty."

"Oh, Tess, am I glad to see you. I'm afraid it didn't go at all well yesterday. The scene Elizabeth made was quite frightening."

Tess nodded. "I know, I know," she said. "Why do you think I'm here in the first place?" She looked around the kitchen. "You got some tomato juice? That's what the patient is going to be looking for. Trust me on that one."

Monica crossed the kitchen and pulled open the door of the refrigerator. Her brow furrowed as she searched the sparsely filled shelves.

"Tomato juice," she said. "I don't think so. I don't think Elizabeth is the tomato-juice type." Monica closed the refrigerator door. "No tomato juice here," she said ruefully.

"Oh, never mind," said Tess. "I'll make it myself." A bottle of chilled tomato juice, a raw egg, a variety of condiments, and a little pot of horseradish seemed to appear from thin air. She went about her task with skill.

"We've got a lot of iced tea around here," said Monica. "It seems to be the beverage of choice."

Tess laughed as she worked up her hangover cure. "That must have been a surprise."

"Why didn't you tell me about her drinking from the start, Tess?" Monica asked. "I couldn't for the life of me figure out what her problem was . . . beautiful, intelligent daughter, darling granddaughter, an interesting career—she's articulate, sophisticated, and funny too. I thought this might have something to do with being lonely, having lost her husband and all. Then I discovered the iced tea . . . I wish I had known in the beginning. You might have given me a hint, at least."

Tess thought for a moment. "Well, when you met Elizabeth, you met the *real* woman. Not the alcoholic. You see, you made friends with a very strong and talented and interesting woman. If you had known back then what you know today, you might have seen the drinker and not the woman." Tess paused a moment to crack the egg on the edge of the glass and to drop it into the drink she was making.

"Alcohol hides a lot of things, Monica. It covers up the real person who is drinking, just as it deadens the drinker. I wanted you to get to know Elizabeth Jessup, the woman. That's who we love, and that's who we want to help here."

"But she doesn't want any help," said Monica. "Believe me, she has made it very clear . . ."

"Then it's up to you to help her to want it," said Tess. "Lead her to the path the Father has for her."

"This could take years," Monica replied. "I don't know Elizabeth well, but I know when she digs in her heels they stay put. This could be a very long assignment."

"You got somewhere to go?" Tess asked.

"It's not that," said Monica. "It's just so terrible to watch her destroy herself like this. It could go on and on . . ."

"Well, think how it looks to her," said Tess. "She's intelligent; do you suppose she thinks what she's doing is normal? Can you imagine how it must feel to wake up and realize that you're killing yourself with each drink? That your family cares about you, but they can't do anything about it? Or how terrible you feel when you've told yourself you'll never drink again . . . and then find you haven't got the willpower to stop, to fight the very thing that is making you and those around you miserable? I've known a lot of drinkers in my time, Monica, and the cycle goes around and around. And they are the only ones who can get themselves off that particularly nasty merry-go-round."

"Oh, Tess, it looks so impossible . . ."

While they were talking, neither Tess nor Monica had noticed that Elizabeth had woken up and was standing in the doorway of the kitchen. She could not see Tess, of course, so as far as she could tell, Monica was standing in her kitchen having a spirited conversation with herself.

"She's back," said Elizabeth, smiling slightly. "My little merry sunshine. And she talks to herself. Just the way I do. This is not comforting, I can tell you that."

Tess did not bother to turn around. "I think I'm going to leave the two of you alone now," she told Monica, who was sorry to see her go. This was just about the time when she could really use some help. But this was her assignment and she would have to find a way. She knew in her heart and soul that nothing was impossible with God.

"Elizabeth," said Monica as brightly as she could manage. "You're up already?"

"I fell asleep," said Elizabeth. "I did not die or slip into a coma."

"I'm sorry . . ."

"Sorry I didn't die or slip into a coma?"

Monica laughed. "No, of course not. Don't be silly. You know what I mean . . ."

Elizabeth walked into the kitchen. Even from a yard or two away, Monica could smell the sour bourbon and stale cigarette smoke. Elizabeth's eyes were bloodshot and red-rimmed, her skin sallow. She looked—and smelled—terrible, but she still wanted Monica to know who was in charge around this house.

"Well, if you insist on being here, Monica, you could make yourself useful."

"Of course," said Monica. "What can I do for you, Elizabeth?"

"I could use a Bloody Mary," Elizabeth replied. "One with a very healthy dose of zip in it."

Monica held up the glass that Tess had been working on. "Well, here's one . . . I'm afraid it's a bit zipless, though." She smiled, wondering if Elizabeth would mind drinking a raw egg in her Bloody Mary. She decided not to ask.

Elizabeth took the glass gratefully, sniffed it and grimaced. "Ew . . . ," she said. "It reminds me of Moscow back in the Gromyko days. A city without zip and a man so boring he wouldn't have known how to spell it, you know?" Elizabeth turned and pulled a bottle of vodka from a shelf and started to unscrew the cap. "This Bloody Mary calls for some pretty major surgery."

Monica took a step toward her and put out her hand to stop her from opening the bottle. "Elizabeth," she said, a look of real concern in her eyes, "don't you ever get tired of feeling this way? Doesn't it make you ill every day? Don't you see what this behavior is doing to you? It'll kill you . . . and you have so much to live for."

The look on Elizabeth's face hardened and her voice was cold. "You know where the door is, Sugar."

"I ask because I care about you," said Monica. She looked down at the floor, hurt by the sting of Elizabeth's words. But no matter how much the words hurt—and even though she knew where the door was—she had no intention of leaving until Elizabeth saw reason.

Elizabeth wasn't quite ready to deal with reality, but she could see that she had hurt Monica's feelings. She took a deep breath and tried to sound calm and rational.

"All right," she said. "I am truly sorry about last night. And I can understand if you're worried about me. But Honey, it looks a lot worse than it is, understand?"

"But Sydney—"

Elizabeth waved dismissively, as if physically pushing her daughter to one side. "Sydney," she said with a little laugh. "What does she know about anything?"

"She sees what's going on," Monica protested. "I think you underestimate her—and her intentions are good. She thinks so much of you."

But Elizabeth was not convinced. "Sydney always overreacts. Monica, I have learned how to drink. I had to."

"Nobody has to do anything like that," Monica insisted. "And as for learning how to drink—"

"Listen to me," said Elizabeth. "When I say I had to learn how to drink I mean it! I *had* to." She tapped the table firmly. "It was not easy being

129

a woman in my business and it still isn't, but believe me, Monica, back when I was starting out it was really a boys' club." She looked Monica hard in the eye. "And if you wanted in—you drank. Understand? Those boys in the foreign press corps—I don't care if it was Moscow or London or Madrid, Saigon, Seoul, Rome, Athens—you name it. When little Miss Jessup started covering the big stories, the guys in the club started to watch her. They were looking for a weakness, a slipup, a mistake. I told you about my welcome to the Saigon Press Club— it was like that everywhere.

"What they really wanted was tears—but I never cried and I never refused to drink. I got into the club. And I was good—as good as any of them . . ." She turned away from Monica and was silent.

"So why do you still do it?" Monica asked. "You don't have to prove anything to anyone anymore."

Elizabeth shrugged but she did not turn

around. "Things change. You get older . . . the idea of getting on a military transport and flying to—I don't know, Bosnia, it's not quite as exciting as it used to be."

She turned and sighed. "The only trouble is, I've had a couple of bad years, so I'm home alone a lot now and . . . okay, maybe I drink a little more than I used to. Sydney sees that and jumps to conclusions." She poured a little vodka into the tomato juice concoction.

"Monica," she said, "you really shouldn't be worrying about it." She took a sip and seemed to shiver. "Ever been to a U.S.-Soviet summit? No, of course you haven't. I covered the Nixon-Brezhnev Strategic Arms meeting in 1972 and a half dozen since then." She took another gulp of her morning drink. "They are the only times I've seen history being made that were boring beyond belief. First their side gets up, makes the Communist spiel, then our side gets up and makes our capitalist spiel . . . then nothing happens while the foreign minister and the secretary of state whisper behind closed doors for a few days, and all of a sudden—Boom! We have a treaty. Like SALT or something."

"Salt?" Monica asked.

"Strategic Arms Limitation Talks," said Elizabeth. "The things that were supposed to save us from nuclear destruction, until we outspent the Soviets and their whole system collapsed. The last one I went to was with Reagan in 1984. The smartest thing I did on that one was to take Sydney with me."

"You took Sydney to Russia?" Monica asked, then added, "Oh, yes, she mentioned that you had done that."

"She was in her element there," said Elizabeth. "I thought that it would give her the bug. I thought after that, she'd want to follow in her old lady's footsteps . . . All the press people loved her—even the Russians. And let me tell you the Russian press corps is about as loving as that refrigerator over there."

"Tell me," said Monica. "What did she do?"

Elizabeth laughed. "She had just started college . . . and how was I supposed to know that she was taking Russian as her foreign language requirement? We arrive in Moscow and all of a sudden my little girl starts speaking the language! I can tell you, I was not prepared for that development. Her Russian wasn't perfect, but it was good enough and the Russians were amazed! Plus, it turns out that she knows everything we were supposed to see in Moscow. Monica, Honey, I'd been there a dozen times before and I never saw anything but the inside of the bar in the Metropole Hotel! But not with Sydney. We went all over the place: Red Square, the Lenin Mausoleum, St. Basil's Cathedral, the Bolshoi, the Tretyakov Gallery . . . She ran me ragged between press briefings. Once I had a little too much vodka and she faced down some pain-in-the-neck cop who wanted to take me to the Moscow version of the pokey. Now *that* took a lot of courage, 'cause those Russian cops do not fool around, believe me. She showed a lot of spunk that day."

Monica nodded. "You admire that."

Elizabeth nodded. "Sure do."

"Well, it took a lot of courage for Sydney to do what she did yesterday too," Monica said forcefully, desperate to get through to her. "She was risking so much, but she was prepared to do it to help you. Standing up to a Russian policeman was probably a lot easier than standing up to you yesterday."

Elizabeth took a long, slow sip of her drink. "Yeah . . . well I am who I am and she still doesn't get it, does she? Besides, I could have handled myself back in Moscow and I can handle myself now. I didn't ask for Sydney's help then. And I'm not asking for it now. Do you understand me, Monica?"

"I understand that Sydney stepped up and helped you without your asking either time."

"She doesn't care," said Elizabeth. "She gave up on me a hundred years ago."

"That's just not true," said Monica. "You know it's not true. Sydney would never have done what she did if she didn't care. And while we're on the subject, little Beth cares very much too."

"Oh, well, you just know everything, don't you, Sugar?" She reached for the vodka bottle and slopped some more of the colorless liquid into her tomato juice. "You show up here—what—yesterday, the day before, and all of a sudden you're an expert on me, my daughter, my granddaughter—my entire family. Just who do you think you are anyway?"

Monica didn't want to argue. "I know that your daughter not only cares about you, but she is proud of you too. She probably stood up to that policeman in Moscow because she couldn't stand to see you humiliated. A little college girl in a foreign country taking on a big policeman. What does that tell you?"

"Huh," said Elizabeth.

"And I wish you could have seen her face the other day," Monica continued.

"What other day?"

"When the mayor was talking about all your awards and achievements. Sydney was so proud of you, she was almost bursting with it. I was watching her. I know."

"Well," said Elizabeth, taking another slug of her Bloody Mary. "She's sure got a funny way of showing it."

"She named her little girl after you, for good- ness 'sake," Monica said. "What more could you ask for?"

"I'm talking about last night," said Elizabeth. "Bringing a rehabilitation counselor in here does not exactly suggest that Sydney is proud of ol' Mom."

"She's showing you that she loves you enough to fight for you," Monica insisted. "Why can't you see through your own pride to see what she is trying to do for you, Elizabeth?"

There was a long silence and although Elizabeth tried hard to hide it, Monica's words had managed to hit their mark. It was the first chink in Elizabeth's stout armor. It was a lot easier for her to change the subject than to face the truth.

"Well," she said finally, "did you come here to work or to gab? I have a lot of stuff for you to look through. I have to take a shower and go out and do some errands . . ."

Elizabeth had just one errand. She was going to go to Sydney's house and deliver the birthday present she had been meaning to give her granddaughter all week. Of course, she also wanted to scout the lay of the land, to get an idea of just how serious Sydney had been in her threats the night before.

After a long, hot shower, a dose of eyedrops, and some carefully applied makeup, there was no resemblance between the smartly dressed Elizabeth reflected in the bedroom mirror and the hungover wreck who had spent the night on the couch.

As Elizabeth drove herself to Sydney's house she wondered how anyone could take her for an alcoholic. Alcoholics were down-and-out losers who only craved that next taste of cheap wine or rotgut gin. She, on the other hand, did her work, kept herself up—and her hands were as steady as rocks. Sure, she liked a drink at the end of the day, but who didn't? It was a little reward for all the hard work the world handed you. Elizabeth managed to forget that on that day she had also *begun* her day with a drink.

She said aloud in the car: "Alcoholic? Me? Ha!"

By the time she arrived at Sydney's modest house she was already good and angry. It was not a good state to be in—not if one was secretly hoping for reconciliation with the two people she loved the most.

Elizabeth parked her car at the curb of Sydney's house, pulled open the door and slammed it forcefully behind her. Quietly fuming, she strode up the front steps and rang the doorbell as if it were a declaration of war. She looked around the neighborhood, like a general surveying the terrain of a forthcoming battle, all the while tapping her foot, waiting for the door to be answered.

Sydney peered suspiciously at her mother through the window in the front door, then summoned all of her courage before warily opening the door.

"Hello, Mother," she said, placing her body between the edge of the door and the frame, blocking the entrance.

Elizabeth had no idea that she would not be welcome to enter her daughter's house. She took a step toward Sydney, but the younger woman barred her way. Elizabeth gazed at Sydney in amazement.

"So I can't come in now?" she said angrily. "I'm not welcome in my own daughter's house?"

"Mother," Sydney said, "I am just trying to help you. You have to understand that."

"Then how about showing me a little kindness," Elizabeth shot back. "How about letting me in?"

"I can't," she replied. "I can't let you in and I cannot put up with what you are doing."

Elizabeth felt the pressure of her anger building and she couldn't keep her voice from rising. "All I'm trying to do is give my granddaughter her birthday gift!"

"And she can't accept it!"

"Well, why don't we ask her?" Elizabeth demanded. "Let's leave it up to her."

Both mother and daughter glanced inside the house to see if Beth was listening.

Sydney lowered her voice almost to a whisper. "Mother, not until you get some help. Some professional help. Until you do, we cannot have anything to do with you. I'm sorry, but that's the way it's going to have to be." Her mind was really made up this time. She would not allow her mother to sweet-talk her way into the house or even into their lives—not as she was now. "I'm truly sorry, really, I am . . ."

"You're sorry?" Elizabeth said. "You're not sorry . . . you're jealous."

Sydney's shoulders slumped. "Oh, please," she said. "You can't really believe—"

"Of course you're jealous," Elizabeth spit. "This is just the stunt your father would have pulled." She was so angry and hurt by her daughter's words and uncompromising way that she almost gave in to her anger and threw Beth's present down on the stone steps. But the gift was the little porcelain angel that played "Amazing Grace" and there was no doubt that the delicate little thing would have shattered. Elizabeth knew that no matter how angry she was at Sydney she could never bring herself to hurt Beth.

Elizabeth stood up as straight as she could, gathered the tatters of her dignity, and looked her daughter in the eye. "Okay, Sydney," she said. "Play your little game . . . But if you think you are going to keep me away from Beth forever, you have another thing coming."

Monica had done exactly as Elizabeth had told her. She had returned to the study to work on the memoirs. The section of manuscript she was working on now was a collection of random notes and documents, old letters and press clippings that were desperately in need of some kind of organization. She started by arranging the clips and letters by date, starting with what appeared to be the oldest and working her way forward to the most current.

The most recent letter she found gave her sudden pause and made her heart ache as she read it. It was a letter from the managing editor of the newspaper that Elizabeth had written countless articles for over the years, her journalistic home. It was dated early in 1991.

. . . sorry to have taken so long to get back to you, but things have been crazy here—as you might imagine. The Pentagon is saying nothing about the Kuwait/Iraq problem, of course, but our back channels have made it clear that there is going to

be a war in the Gulf and it's going to happen soon. Of course, I don't have to tell you that, Elizabeth, you old newshound—you figured the situation out weeks ahead of us all, I'll bet.

As for sending you to the Gulf, I've talked it over with the editorial board and we all agree that the Gulf War is probably not the assignment for you. You've covered your share of shot and shell, Elizabeth, why not sit this one out and let some of the new kids get some experience? If this changes or anything comes up that we think might be suitable for you, we'll let you know . . .

Monica knew what this meant. It meant that Elizabeth Jessup had been put out to pasture . . .

Chapter Eight

Elizabeth pulled open the creaky sliding double doors that led to one of the rooms of the house, laughing as the old wood groaned and squeaked on the brass rollers.

"This old house is falling apart," she said with a chuckle. "Sort of like its owner."

"They both have character," said Monica, following her into the room.

"I call this the library," Elizabeth said. "It sounds grand, but I know it looks like a dump."

There were floor-to-ceiling bookshelves, all of them crammed with books and papers. The old mahogany library table could barely be seen under the massive pile of papers. It looked like the aftermath of an avalanche.

"My personal filing system," said Elizabeth, glancing at the stack of papers.

"I know," said Monica.

"That's right," Elizabeth replied. "I forgot You are already familiar with my filing system." She stopped in the middle of the room, her hands on her hips, looking at all the things crammed into the room. "I guess I should call it my trophy room too."

The library walls were decorated similarly to the rooms in the rest of the house. The walls that weren't covered by bookshelves were lined with plaques and awards, scrolls and certificates, as well as a series of photographs: Elizabeth with President Lyndon Johnson, Elizabeth with Martin Luther King Jr., Elizabeth with a host of famous people, mostly figures in politics and diplomacy.

But one picture stood out from the others: a shot of Elizabeth hunched down wearing full camouflage, a "boonie hat" on her head. Monica could see that she was following a patrol of American infantrymen making their way through a piece of dense, dark Vietnamese jungle.

"You were in Vietnam?" Monica asked. "I didn't know you were in combat."

Elizabeth laughed and lit a cigarette. "Sure I was in Vietnam. Honey, Vietnam was my very first war. And I did many others after that one— that is, if you consider Granada and Panama wars."

"But you went into combat with the troops?" Monica asked as she studied the photograph closely.

Elizabeth sucked in on her cigarette and laughed the smoke out. "You go where the story is, Sweetie, and the story was out where the fighting was." She inhaled again. "There was no point trying to report a war from Saigon. The State Department and the army wouldn't give you any straight dope."

"Were you ever under fire?" Monica asked. "I mean, did anyone ever shoot at you?"

"Sure . . ." Elizabeth laughed again. "But they weren't shooting at me," she said. "At least, I didn't take it personally."

Monica shook her head slowly. It was hard to imagine that this woman could be so fearless in the face of exceptional danger, but a coward when it came to facing the battles and insecurities within herself. It seemed that for some people, getting shot at was easier to bear than examining one's own faults and shortcomings.

"I didn't just report from the ground," Elizabeth explained. "I flew with the air force, the marines, and the army air cav—that's the cavalry. Only they've taken away their horses and given them helicopters now, but they're still cowboys at heart."

Monica laughed. "I can't imagine it . . . still it must have been safer in the air than on the ground."

"Right," said Elizabeth with mock indignance. She rooted around in the debris on the desk and came up with an orange handle attached to a length of heavy-duty, woven stainless steel cable about a half inch thick.

"Any idea what this is?" she asked, handing the object to Monica, who turned it over in her hands. The words "United States Navy" were stenciled in thick black letters on the handle.

"I haven't the slightest idea," Monica said. "Something of a military nature."

"Military nature . . ." Elizabeth laughed again. "You might say that. That thing is the pin from my ejection seat. I happened to have it in my hand when I finally hit the ground . . ."

Monica's eyes widened. "Elizabeth, what on earth were you doing? What happened?"

"I was flying with a squadron of Intruders based on an aircraft carrier in the Gulf of Tonkin. I went on a raid to Hanoi and we took a lot of ground fire—lost about half of our undercarriage. There was no way to land that thing. The pilot asked me if I wanted to punch out over land or in the water." She chuckled again. "After he explained that punch out was a nice way of saying ejecting, we both chose dry land." She shrugged. "So out we went," she relayed matter-of-factly. "The Navy let me keep the pin. They said it was the least I deserved."

"Amazing," said Monica.

"All in a day's work," she said. "Well," she added briskly, "I think it's time for a little iced tea . . ."

Monica looked down and said nothing, but it was plain that Elizabeth could read volumes in the small gesture. She eyed Monica for a moment and folded her arms across her chest.

"You think Sydney's right, don't you?" she said after a moment or two.

Monica nodded. "Yes, I do," she said.

Elizabeth's voice was low and soft. "Well, if I want to see Beth I guess I have to . . . play along. I'll have to show up at a . . . meeting or . . . something." She looked up at Monica, the old Elizabeth gleam in her eye. "Just for the record, however, I want you to know that I deeply resent this."

"Noted," said Monica with a little smile.

"Good . . ." Elizabeth shrugged, as if resigned to her fate. "I guess I better find the business card that woman left here last night. That silly card I threw away . . ." Elizabeth had no recollection whatsoever of having ripped the card to shreds the night before. But Monica had a solution.

She produced a fresh business card with the phone number for Anita, the counselor at the New Hope Center. "Here it is," she said.

Elizabeth took it from her and studied it. "She must have been dropping these things around here like bread crumbs." She squared her shoulders and started for the door. "All right . . . Ready or not, here I come."

Monica smiled happily and tossed the pin back onto Elizabeth's already cluttered desk. Getting Elizabeth out the door was not much, but she had to be grateful for small victories and hope that they would eventually add up and win the war . . .

151

Monica's hope was short-lived. In the few minutes it took to drive to the New Hope Center, Elizabeth had built up a serious wall of defense to combat the feeling that she was being forced to do something against her will.

The setup at the center did not do much to help. It was housed in a run-down church hall very much on the wrong side of the railroad tracks in Elizabeth's little town. The people there, the recovering alcoholics, did not impress her much either.

"Look at them," she said, glancing at the crowd of people gathered around the coffee urn. Among them was Anita. "This is just pathetic, isn't it?"

"They're here to get help just like you are," said Monica. But she knew that Elizabeth was being critical to hide her own fear and uneasiness.

A middle-aged man approached them, a big smile on his face. "Howdy," he said. "We'll be starting real soon, so why don't you just take a seat, okay?"

"Thank you," said Monica. When he had left, she whispered to Elizabeth, "Well, he seemed nice enough."

"Reminds me too much of kindergarten," Elizabeth said. "You know what I mean?" She glanced around the room. "Too many bright smiling faces, if you ask me."

She reached into her shoulder bag and pulled out her elegant gold cigarette case and cigarette lighter. She thrust the cigarette into her mouth and lit it.

Almost instantly a woman pounced on her. She wore as big a grin as the man who had spoken to them, but her message was not quite as benign. "I'm sorry," she said. "This is a non-smoking meeting. I'm afraid you'll have to put that out."

Elizabeth scowled at her. "You have got to be kidding," she said in a deadpan voice.

"There are smokers' meetings," the woman said. "They're listed in the directory. I'll go and get you one."

Elizabeth watched her go and then spat out one word. "Fascist!" she said.

"Oh, Elizabeth, please . . . ," said Monica. "Please try to go along with this. Just give it a chance."

But she was in no mood to be placated by Monica.

"Don't 'Oh, Elizabeth' me," she replied. "You see all this here?"

She waved her cigarette, leaving an arc of smoke in the air. "This is why I didn't want to get involved in this sort of thing. They want to dictate every detail of your life to get you well. Well, I say forget them." She let out a pall of smoke and then turned on her heel, making for the door as quickly as she could.

Anita cut her off before she reached the exit. "Elizabeth," she said, "I am so glad you are here. I know it took a lot of courage to come here today."

Elizabeth turned and looked at Anita, her cigarette held up, plain to see. "Well, look who's here," she said. "I've been doing a lot of thinking about our first meeting."

"That's good," said Anita.

"Maybe you should wait to hear what I've been thinking about before you start congratulating yourself." Elizabeth's tone of voice had turned ugly. "There's something that I really want to tell you. Is that okay with you?"

"Okay," Anita replied uncertainly. "Sure . . ."

"If you ever come to my house again . . . I will personally rip out your arms and use them to play you like a marimba. How dare you try to turn my family against me!"

Anita had been through this sort of thing a dozen times before and she firmly and compassionately stood her ground. "I understand," she said. "I understand your anger, Elizabeth."

But the gentle words seemed to make Elizabeth even angrier. "You don't understand oatmeal," she shouted. "And if I ever catch you near me or near them again, I will get a restraining order against you and I will sue for harassment and assault!" There was an uncomfortable silence in the hall and people were watching Elizabeth now. She didn't care but knew she had to make something of a showy exit.

"Now come on," she commanded Monica. "I'm in the mood for a little champagne . . ." She swept toward the door then stopped. Monica was not following.

"Well, Monica, are you coming?" Elizabeth demanded. "Or are you going to stay here with these . . . zombies?"

Monica shook her head slowly and gave her an imploring look, as if begging her not to leave. "I'm sorry, Elizabeth . . ."

Elizabeth shrugged as if it hardly mattered. "Well . . . I guess this means you're fired then, doesn't it."

Monica nodded. "I guess it does," she said sadly.

Chapter Nine

*E*lizabeth meant it when she said she was in the mood for champagne. On the way home she stopped at a liquor store and bought two big bottles of good French champagne—she spent more than she intended, but she really didn't care—and then went home and set about drinking both of them.

She did not, however, pop them open the minute she walked in the door. First, she decided to set the scene a little. She got a good champagne flute from the cabinet and washed it out, gathered her cigarettes and a clean ashtray, and then settled in her study.

The moment called for a little music and she riffled through her extensive collection of records. She silently debated the relative merits of Bessie Smith, Billie Holiday, and Lena Horne and then settled on Billie Holiday because her voice suited Elizabeth's mood: dark and downtrodden. She had the blues and Billie Holiday's record was the perfect music for feeling sorry for yourself.

She settled in an armchair, popped open the first bottle of champagne, poured herself a glass, and drank. As Billie Holiday's smoky voice mixed with the cigarette haze hanging in the air, Elizabeth nursed her sense of injured pride. But she did not nurse her drinks. The first bottle went quickly and, without hesitation, she opened the second.

"I understand your anger, Elizabeth," she sneered, quoting Anita. "That woman doesn't know a thing about me. Or anything she knows she got from Sydney!"

She topped off her glass and listened to Billie Holiday sing "Lover Man." Elizabeth thought of her own husband, whom she had divorced so many years ago. She had no idea where he had gone. And when she thought about the death of Sydney's husband, she felt even gloomier.

"I'll tell you why I drink," she announced to the silent room. "Because I'm bored . . ." Then she sighed, and forced herself to add, "And I'm lonely, too."

When Beth turned seven years of age she earned the very grave responsibility of being allowed to walk home from school without parental supervision. Sydney didn't worry about this too much as the school was only a little over a block from home, and she knew her daughter would walk home with three of her friends who lived nearby.

What Sydney did not know was that on that particular day Beth would break away from her friends and take a different route home—one that led her right by her grandmother's house. When the little girl got to Elizabeth's house she stood on the pavement outside, wondering what she should do. She was not quite sure what the source of the trouble was between her mother and her grandmother, but she knew it was really serious.

After Elizabeth had tried to visit the other day, Sydney knew she had to give Beth some kind of explanation. The little girl loved her grandmother so much she had to be given a reason why she could not see her for a while.

Sydney had done her best not to frighten the little girl. She sat her down in the living room and stroked her hair. Beth gazed at her, her face still and solemn.

"Bethie, you understand that Grandma is having a lot of trouble right now."

Beth nodded. "Uh-huh . . ."

"It's like she's sick," Sydney said, groping for the right words to explain the dilemma.

"Why doesn't she go to the doctor?" Beth asked. "That's what you're supposed to do, isn't it?"

Sydney nodded. "That's right. That's the whole problem. She won't go to the doctor and it's up to us to see that she goes and gets well again."

"Can you take her?" the little girl asked.

"No," said Sydney, shaking her head. "She has to go herself. Until she wants to go, she won't get well. And until she goes by herself, we can't see her."

This did not make a lot of sense to the little girl. "Because we might catch what she has?"

Sydney smiled. "No, that's not it. It's hard to explain, but we'll be helping her by *not* seeing her."

"But I miss her," said Beth.

"We both do," her mother replied.

Beth turned this conversation around in her mind as she looked at the front door of Elizabeth's house. She was not, by nature, a disobedient girl and she didn't want to let her mother down, but the simple fact was she wanted to see her grandmother.

So, without further hesitation, she raced up the steps and knocked on the front door.

Elizabeth was well into the second bottle of champagne and feeling the effects of the alcohol. She wasn't so far gone, however, that she didn't hear the knocking at the door.

"I'm coming," she whispered.

Wearily, she put down her glass and dragged herself out of her chair. With a slight stagger she made for the door, cigarette in hand. She did not know for sure who her visitor might be, but she was pretty sure it was Monica coming to beg for her job back. Her publishers would not be pleased if she didn't get her manuscript in order and she could hardly go back to the office without it in hand. Of course, right then, Elizabeth didn't care about what she imagined to be Monica's problems because she was so caught up in her own.

She was, however, delighted to see her grand-daughter standing at her front door.

"Ah, Bethie," Elizabeth sighed through a cloud of cigarette smoke. "Decided to take a risk and cross enemy lines, did you?" Beth threw her arms around her grandmother's waist and squeezed her tight. Elizabeth felt a great flood of mater-nal love but a stab of conscience at the same time. She was very pleased that Beth had shown her mettle by daring to visit—it was just the kind of thing *she* would have done at the same age—but she also knew that Beth was disobeying her mother and with Sydney's tendency to worry, she knew she had to get her granddaughter home before her mother called the police.

Elizabeth walked Beth into the house. "Come on in. Come in . . . Now you know you're sup-posed to go straight home after school, don't you? I can just imagine how worried your mother must be. I'll bet she's having a heart attack." She looked at her granddaughter and did her best to appear stern and disapproving. "Now you know as well as I do you aren't supposed to be here."

Beth looked up at Elizabeth, her brown eyes big and trusting. "But I missed you," she said simply.

Elizabeth's attempt at being severe and strict melted under Beth's gaze and loving words.

There was no defense against the purity of a child's love and Elizabeth was profoundly moved. The effects of more than a bottle and a half of champagne and the self-pity had already made her close to being weepy, but she fought to control her emotions. It was not easy, but she managed to pull it off well enough. Beth did not recognize that anything was wrong; Grandma was always sort of like that.

"Bethie . . . okay . . . um, this is what I'll do. I'll make you a deal . . ."

Beth smiled sweetly. "Okay."

Elizabeth walked through the hallway and into the house proper. She went to the glass-fronted cabinet that contained a number of treasures she had gathered in her travels and pulled open the door.

"Come here, Beth . . . you see this?" She picked up the porcelain angel that Beth loved so much.

"Uh-huh," said Beth. "That's my angel."

Elizabeth nodded and grinned. "That's *right*," she said emphatically. "It is yours. I want you to have it."

"Really?" Bethie asked. "Mine. To take home?"

"It's your favorite, isn't it?" Elizabeth asked.

"Uh-huh," said Beth, nodding.

"Okay. Then you take it home with you," Elizabeth replied. And even through her alcohol-induced haze, Elizabeth knew that she had to do something to get Beth home before Sydney went crazy.

She was smart enough to realize that she was in no condition to drive Beth home herself—a DWI was the last thing she needed—so it seemed inevitable that she would have to call her daughter, something she had quietly sworn never to do again. She sighed heavily. She was not looking forward to this. But all of a sudden, she felt terribly tired.

"You take your little angel, Honey," said Elizabeth. "Then I'm going to give your mother a call . . . and you can go home with her, okay?"

"Thank you," said Beth. "Will you fix it that Mommy isn't mad at me for coming here?"

Elizabeth laughed a little and blinked her heavy-lidded eyes. "Don't worry, Honey. Believe me—you are *not* the one your mother is going to be mad at. I know that for a fact." She pulled open the sliding double doors that led into the library. "All right, Sweetie. Why don't you come on in here and . . ." For a moment Elizabeth's mind went blank. "Come in here and watch the news on television."

Beth grimaced. The evening news was not exactly high on the seven-year-old girl's "must watch" list. "Grandma, do I have to watch the news?"

"Sure you do," Elizabeth replied. "You don't

want to grow up to be just another uninformed citizen, do you?"

Beth shook her head. "Uh-uh."

"All right," said Elizabeth, ushering her into the room. "Come on." She sat her granddaughter down in the big armchair facing the television set and turned it on. "Just don't make it too loud, okay? I've got a bad headache."

She closed the double doors of the room and wandered through the house, puffing on her cigarette. She knew she should call Sydney immediately, but somehow she just was not up to facing her daughter's holier-than-thou attitude that drove Elizabeth crazy.

She sank into the couch in the living room and leaned back, resting her neck on the top edge. Her head was spinning and her mouth was dry. She had taken in too much alcohol in too little time. Sitting there on the couch, Elizabeth didn't so much fall asleep as simply pass out. A moment or two after she slipped into unconsciousness, the cigarette in her right hand fell out of her fingers and into a pile of that day's newspapers scattered on the floor at her feet. The cigarette rolled a couple of inches before getting caught in a fold of newsprint.

It took only a few seconds for the pages of the newspaper to begin to smolder, and soon the red glow of flame appeared, small at first, but growing quickly. It did not take long to consume the pile of newspaper and the fire moved on to more substantial fuel, spreading across the carpet to the drapes on the window, the flames racing toward the ceiling.

Beth was doing exactly what she had been told to do, dutifully watching the local news, attempting to understand something called "a bond issue" that the mayor seemed to believe in very passionately. She had no idea what he was talking about—and she had no idea that her life was in terrible danger. It would take a few more minutes before the fire made its way across the house, until it was licking at the double doors of the study.

The smoke was enough to suffocate Elizabeth in her stupor, to kill her before she had the chance to wake up. If there was hidden blessing in this catastrophe it was that the fire got very hot, very quickly and it was the heat on her face that pulled Elizabeth back to consciousness. The mixture of the smoke and the lingering effects of the alcohol made her weak and disoriented. She had completely forgotten that Beth had stopped in to visit and was still in the other room obediently watching the evening news.

The smoke in her chest was sharp and painful, stabbing her lungs like hot needles. Elizabeth found herself gasping for breath, coughing hard. Her ears filled with the crackling roar of the fire and she was oblivious to everything except the need for air.

She staggered through the living room, finding her way more on instinct and fuzzy memory than anything else. Somehow, she made it to the hall without collapsing from smoke inhalation or getting caught in a web of flame. She threw open the front door and the fresh air hit her like a pail of ice water. Stumbling across the porch, she fell through the screen door and onto the grass in front of the house. Then she passed out, her brain fading to black. She did not hear the sirens, nor did she hear her own granddaughter's impassioned cries for help . . .

Just about the time the weather came on the news, Beth noticed the smoke creeping under the doors. She jumped to her feet and ran to the sliding doors. They were very hot to the touch and she could make out the orange line of fire between them.

"Grandma! Grandma!" Bethie cried. "Help me, Grandma! Please! Help me!" There were tears in her eyes and the smoke was making her cough. She pounded on the door, but the heat burned her little hands. She summoned up all the breath she could manage and tried shouting one more time. "Grandma! Grandma! Grandma! Grandma! *Please! Please help me . . .*"

But her Grandma did not come. Beth looked around the room, but could see nothing through the smoke. She dropped to her knees and crawled under a table, her tiny body racked with coughs as she curled herself into a ball. The last thought she had before she lost consciousness was bewildering: *Why hasn't Grandma come to save me?*

Monica did not hear Beth's cries for help, she felt them deep inside her, a sickening feeling that the small child was in grave danger. Beth was close to death—and Monica knew from the Father that it was not yet the little girl's time to go home. One thing was certain: Monica had to save her.

When Monica appeared in front of Elizabeth's house, the building was almost completely engulfed in flames. Elizabeth was sprawled on the grass. Monica glanced at her, knowing she'd be okay—it was Beth who was the focus of her attention.

Without hesitation Monica walked up the steps and into the burning house. The flames were all around her, but the heat had no effect on her.

She found Beth unconscious in her hiding place, the fire moving relentlessly toward her. Her breathing was shallow and labored, her eyes rolled back in her head, her body limp in Monica's arms as she lifted her.

Monica stood with the little girl cradled in her arms. In the few seconds it had taken to get into the building and to locate Beth, the fire had doubled in intensity. Beyond the sliding double doors of the study she could see that the center hall had become an inferno, a maelstrom of vicious, hot flames that would cause serious harm if they tried to force their way through.

But Monica knew what to do. She turned her face toward the blackened, smoke-filled ceiling of the room, and seemed to be able to see through it to the clear and starry night, the canopy of the heavens over the earth. Monica prayed for guidance and for the safety of the little girl in her arms. The flames crackled for a moment longer, then fell back, opening a path from the study to the front door, much like the parting of the Red Sea. Monica smiled and thanked God, putting all her heart into her prayer of gratitude.

Then she stepped into the passage that God had cleared, walking between the flames without a moment of hesitation. The heat from the fire buffeted her like wind but not a single tongue of flame singed so much as a hair on her head or on Beth's. With God's help, Monica carried her precious charge to safety, out into the fresh air of the cool night.

A crowd had gathered on the far side of the street, the neighbors standing and staring as the fire danced up to the roof of Elizabeth's house. There were gasps from some of them when Monica came out of the burning home.

Fire engines and ambulances were just pulling

up to the curb as Monica emerged from the flames. The first squad of firemen approaching the house saw her coming out of the flame-engulfed structure unscathed and stopped dead in their tracks.

"Lady, where did you come from?" a fireman asked. He *thought* he had seen this woman walk right out of the flames.

"From in there," said Monica. "I think this little girl is badly hurt. Her name is Beth." She surrendered the little girl to an emergency medical technician who had come running up with a stethoscope and a bottle of oxygen. Monica immediately recognized the technician as Andrew, the Angel of Death. He nodded briefly to Monica then focused all of his attention on the fragile little girl that lay before him. Monica, confident that Beth was receiving the best of care, began to walk away.

"Hold it!" yelled one of the firemen. "Lady! You should get yourself checked out too."

"There's no need," said Monica. "I didn't

get hurt at all. The little girl is the one who needs help, as does her grandmother over there." The firemen looked at Elizabeth, who was still in the same spot on the lawn. "Please don't worry about me." And then she seemed to fade into the night . . .

Inside the house the pages of Elizabeth's memoirs crackled and burned, fiery pages floating on currents of heated air. They curled and turned to ash.

Chapter Ten

*E*lizabeth had no idea how she got to the hospital, or why she was there.

To the best of her memory, she was listening to Billie Holiday and drinking champagne, thinking about . . . well, she didn't really remember what she had been thinking about . . . but then there had been a lot of smoke and heat. Other than that she recalled nothing at all. She had no recollection of Beth's unexpected visit, no recollection of sitting down on the living room couch; she did not remember passing out. She had no idea she had caused the fire with her own cigarette. For all Elizabeth knew, there had been an electrical short somewhere, a broken gas valve, or perhaps the house had been struck by lightning.

She was still woozy from all the smoke she had inhaled and she was still a little drunk from the champagne, but she knew one thing for sure: she hated hospitals and doctors and wanted to get out of there as soon as possible.

The doctor on assignment in the emergency room had listened to her heart and lungs, given her sinuses an unpleasant but cleansing saline flush, and had left her to recover on a gurney in one of the curtained cubicles of the emergency room ward.

"You just take it easy here for a minute," the doctor had said. "I'll look in on you in a little while."

"Sure," said Elizabeth, laying back on the thin pillows. "Whatever you say, Doctor." The lie came easy to her.

As soon as the doctor had left the room,

Elizabeth swung her legs off the gurney and sat upright. Her head reeled and she coughed deeply—and she almost lay down again, but she was determined to get out of that place. She knew she would be perfectly fine if she just rested for a minute or two.

She was still sitting on the edge of the high hospital bed looking around the room for her shoes when the doctor returned. The doctor did not expect to see her patient sitting up and looking as if she were about to make her escape.

"Hey, hey, hey," she said. "Not so fast, Ms. Jessup. Where do you think you're going?"

"Home," said Elizabeth.

"I'm not altogether sure how much of a home you have left," said the doctor. "As I understand it from the fire department, the damage was pretty extensive. I know you're worried about your house and want to see it, but if I were you, I wouldn't go home tonight. I have to tell you that would be a mistake."

Elizabeth Jessup fixed her cold stare on the

doctor. "If I cannot go home," she said, "I will go elsewhere. The point is, I am not staying in this place one minute longer. Do you understand me? I am definitely going to get out of here. Now." She tried to climb down from the bed, but she swayed unsteadily.

"Look," said the doctor, "you got a little smoke inhalation. It isn't really serious, but it's enough that I strongly recommend you spend a night here."

"I am not interested in your recommendation," Elizabeth said, her words slurred, her voice low. "I told you already, I want out of this place right now. I do not want to spend another minute here. Why is this not getting through to you?"

The doctor did her best to make this headstrong woman understand. "Ms. Jessup," she said. "You have had a considerable shock to your system this evening. You should not leave the ER in this condition."

"You said it was not serious. Goodnight . . ." Elizabeth managed to get off the bed this time.

"And if you don't tell me where my shoes are I am quite prepared to walk out of here barefoot."

"They are in the locker under your bed," the doctor said quickly. "I said it was not serious, but you have had a shock to your heart and lungs. One night of observation of your condition would make a world of difference. You'll feel much, much better in the morning if you'll just stay the night."

Elizabeth dug out her shoes and slipped them on her feet. "Oh, Honey," she said, almost laughing at the doctor. "I have had some conditions, and believe me, this is not one of them." Elizabeth stood upright and squared her shoulders as best she could. She looked as if she had something very important to say, as if she were about to deliver a timely speech.

"Now, Doc, I do not have the slightest idea how I got in here in the first place, but I can tell you how I'm going to leave . . ." She pointed. "I'm walking straight through that door. And I'm going to do it right now. Thank you for your time and effort, Doc. But let me tell you, I'm really not worth it." She started toward the door.

"Look," said the doctor, desperate to get her to stay. "Look, just stay overnight, just for observation. Ms. Jessup, it cannot hurt and it could do you some good."

Elizabeth smiled. "You want to observe me." She turned and threw her arms apart. "So observe . . . take a good look." She paused for a moment.

"Now observe me saying good-bye, Doctor." And she walked out of the room, leaving the doctor speechless.

Elizabeth would rather have died than admit it, but she was absolutely delighted to see Sydney. Her daughter was pacing nervously in the waiting room, her face pale, her mouth set in a tight line. She had rushed out of the house in a pair of old blue jeans and a T-shirt, her long dark hair in tangles. She knew she looked terrible, but she didn't care one way or the other.

When she saw her mother stumbling down the hall she stopped and folded her arms across her chest and stared at her. She did not look happy to see her, but Elizabeth did not notice Sydney's icy glare.

"So you care after all," said Elizabeth with a glazed smile. "I knew you did, deep down."

Sydney did not budge an inch. "I guess I should have known that *you'd* be the one walking out of this place under her own power. That's just like you."

For a moment, Elizabeth thought she was getting a compliment from her daughter. "I'm a survivor, Sydney," she said. "You could have been one, too, if you had let me teach you how. There's a skill to always coming out alive." She smiled at her daughter again. "But I've done all the surviving I plan on doing tonight. Sydney, be a dear and drive me home. I have no idea how I got here."

Sydney shook her head slowly and her eyes narrowed. "I should have known you'd be drunk. Not even you would have let this happen if you had been sober."

Elizabeth closed her eyes and rubbed her temples. "Sydney, please. I don't need a lecture right now. It was good of you to be concerned, it was very nice of you to come. Thank you." She stumbled a little. "Now would you please . . . just take me home."

She would not admit it of course, but she would have killed for a nice big glass of her special iced tea. She hoped that much of her house still existed—because she doubted that Sydney, given her mood and her current anti-drinking campaign, would stop at a liquor store on the way home and loan her the price of a bottle of scotch.

Sydney's words were as thin and as sharp as razor blades. "I can't believe it," she said. "Not even from you. I would have thought that even *you* would have had some conscience about this."

Elizabeth shot her daughter a withering glance. "Conscience about what? It was my house that burned down, Sweetheart. That's my problem. I'll deal with it. I won't dare to intrude in your precious, safe little world."

Sydney stared at her mother, not quite able to understand what was going on. "You have no idea what has happened, do you? You are completely, drunkenly oblivious, aren't you?"

Elizabeth may have been drunk and half-suffocated, her clothes soot-streaked and stained with grass, but she was not going to allow her daughter to talk to her in that disrespectful manner. "You will not take that tone with me, Sydney."

It was all Sydney could do to restrain herself. She wanted to scream hysterically at her mother, she wanted to lash out and hit her, so Elizabeth would have hurt the way she was hurting. It was with every fiber of her being that Sydney managed to keep herself and her blazing white hot anger in check.

"Didn't anyone tell you what happened tonight?" She threw up her hands. "I can't believe you have no idea what happened. You think this is all about you and your house!"

"Well," Elizabeth mumbled, "there was a fire. I don't know how it started . . . it could have been a radiator, a fuse. It could have been the furnace. It could have been . . ." She stopped, her mind completely befuddled. "Remember last year when I had work done on the furnace—they never got it right, you know. I think they may have a lawsuit—"

"You don't know," Sydney snapped, "because you were drunk. A neighbor saw somebody carry Beth out just in time. And you know what, Mother? That person was not you. They found you passed out—outside on the lawn." Sydney laughed harshly. "Are you a survivor? You bet you are, Mother. *You* got out of that house. But you left my baby to die inside that house."

The words hit Elizabeth like a blow to the gut and for once she staggered, but not from the effects of the drinks. She sucked in air and stared at her daughter.

"Beth? Bethie was there? At the house?" She could not remember her granddaughter being there. No matter how hard she tried she could not bring back that memory. She was almost afraid to ask the next question, but she had to.

"Is she . . . is Bethie all right?" she asked, her voice quavering.

"No," snapped Sydney. "No, she's not all right. She is unconscious. She took in a lot of smoke. She . . . she . . . she's not responding to sound or anything. No one knows if she'll come out of it and if she'll be all right when she does. Thick smoke like that cuts off oxygen to the brain. It could have been toxic."

"Oh, God," Elizabeth whispered. She felt sick to her stomach. This time Sydney was right—this whole catastrophe could only be laid at her feet. And her drinking. There was no escaping the conclusion and, for Elizabeth, it was a sobering thought—literally. In an instant, her head seemed to clear and she could see things with a new and unexpected sense of clarity.

She started toward her daughter, her arms out. "Oh, Sydney, I am so sorry. I—"

Sydney jumped back. "No, no, no," she cried. "From now on you leave us alone." And then, before Elizabeth could say a word, her daughter stormed down the hospital corridor, without a backward glance, determined to walk out of Elizabeth's life once and for all.

Chapter Eleven

 he next hour or so was pure agony for Elizabeth. It was her turn to pace back and forth in the waiting room. Except Elizabeth was not waiting for anything. She knew that no one would be coming out to give her an update on her granddaughter's condition, for as far as the hospital was concerned she was nobody, not a factor in the life-and-death struggle of her granddaughter.

She had watched a little girl die once, in Vietnam. It was while she had been touring a civilian hospital with Brian, her photographer, walking from bed to bed, examining each broken body lying there as if looking at exhibits in a museum of misery. By that time, both she and her photographer had seen plenty of death in Vietnam—they had seen dead Americans, dead Vietcong, dead civilians—and they had become hardened to it. They knew they had to be calloused to the suffering around them, otherwise their jobs would drive them crazy. Neither of them had wanted to tour that hospital, but they were doing it as a favor to a nun she knew, in hopes that it might generate a story, which might, in turn, generate some donations. The hospital lacked almost everything except beds and bandages. The little girl had been bandaged from head to toe—she had been a victim of a napalm attack and even Elizabeth, so accustomed to horrible death, felt a piece of her heart break off when she saw that little girl suffering through the last moments of her life. She could not take her eyes from that small, scarred face, a face that was contorted with pain one moment, then at rest and peaceful a moment later. Elizabeth had never written the article. She could not bring herself to do so. Instead she wrote a big check and made every member of the Press Club write one too. It was not even a story she planned to put in her memoirs.

Now she was reliving it. But this time it was her own flesh and blood, her precious Beth . . .

After a while, she decided that she had felt sorry for herself long enough. It was time to be the Elizabeth Jessup of old, the take-charge, no-nonsense Elizabeth. But this time, she was going to do it right, she was not going to step on any toes.

She walked down the hall in search of her daughter and granddaughter. Midway down the corridor she found them. She peered through the window in the doorway and the sight made her heart cry out in agony.

Beth was lying on a hospital bed, unnaturally still on the green sheets. Strapped to her face was a huge oxygen mask, a piece of equipment so large it obscured Beth's little face from chin to brow. Her chest rose and sank rhythmically, but that was the only movement in the room, except the bellows of the oxygen pump. Slumped on the side of the bed, her head resting on the covers, was Sydney. She was still, too, but her hands were stretched out in front of her, clasped together in prayer.

"Oh, Honey," Elizabeth whispered and tears sprang into her eyes. All she wanted to do was rush into that room and gather her two babies up in her arms. She wanted to squeeze them tight, she wanted to tell them how much she loved them, she wanted to hold them and never, ever let them go. But she knew she could not do that. She was no longer welcome in her family, even in this time of extreme crisis—and it was all her own fault.

Elizabeth backed away from the door slowly and stumbled down the corridor blindly, stopping to lean against the institutional-green cinder-block wall. She was crying hard now— weeping for her little Beth, who was fighting for her life, because of Elizabeth's own carelessness. She was crying for her daughter whom she had hurt time and time again, but who had never turned on her—until now. Curiously, the one person for whom she was not crying—for once— was herself. Without thinking about it, as if it were almost a reflex reaction to a sudden aware- ness of a greater, more powerful being, Elizabeth put her hands together in prayer and looked up. Above her was nothing more than the tiles of the hospital corridor, but Elizabeth wanted, *oh, how she wanted*, to see the heavens up there.

She swallowed deeply and tried to collect her thoughts. "Okay . . . okay . . . okay . . ." Her chin trembled, but she was determined to get this prayer out. "If You can hear me," she whis- pered, "this is Elizabeth . . . and . . . uh . . ." She stopped again, trying to bridle her emotions. Then the words poured out of her in a rush. "If You are really there, I can't imagine why You would want to listen to me, but Kissinger always said, 'Don't waste time with the middleman, go to the top.'"

Then, abruptly, the words stopped. The tears

were rolling down her cheeks and her throat felt
tight and dry. There was no harder thing for
Elizabeth Jessup to ask than what she was about
to ask for. She had always lived her life thinking
that she did not need help from anyone, that she
would always get by on her own nerves, her own
instincts, her own strengths. Her weaknesses she
had hidden, but now they were out in the open
and she needed guidance and support—she needed
to ask God for something she had never asked
any human being for.

"So . . . ," she said, almost choking on her
words, "I could . . . I could really use some help
here . . ."

As she cried and prayed, a nurse in surgical
scrubs passed by. She didn't even glance at
Elizabeth. The woman was singing quietly to
herself in a rich, sonorous voice.

"Amazing grace, how sweet the sound," the
nurse sang, "that saved a wretch like me . . ." Of
course, Elizabeth had no way of knowing that
the nurse was Tess and that no one else in the

hospital would have been able to see her. The message of the song was just what she needed to hear, and for the first time in her life, it struck a chord in a deep place within her heart.

When Elizabeth heard that voice, it seemed to flow through her like a rushing wind and it gave her enough strength to consider what to do next. She wiped her eyes and walked down the corridor to a nurses' station, where two women were working.

One of the nurses turned to her. "Yes, ma'am? Can I help you with something?"

"I've heard that when a person is in a coma . . . I think I read somewhere—that they can hear what's going on around them. Is that true?"

The nurse nodded. "Sometimes. Not always, but sometimes. But in the past I've had several patients on this ward who have responded to voices, music that is very familiar to them—" The nurse smiled. "We even had one that responded to the voices of characters on a soap opera she used to watch day after day."

195

Elizabeth nodded. "Thank you." She left the hospital in a hurry. She knew what she had to do.

Her house was in ruins. Scorched pieces of her furniture had been thrown out onto the patch of lawn in front of the house, most of the windows had been smashed to let smoke and gases escape from the interior, beams from the old wooden attic had fallen through the ceiling and lay sodden in the middle of the house.

Elizabeth stood behind police-barrier tape for a moment, looking at the devastation. There had been a time when those four charred walls had contained a life and a lifetime of memories. The mementos of her life had mostly perished in the blaze—she would probably be able to salvage some of her papers and books, but that would come later and was of no concern to her now. She slipped under the tape printed with the stern warning not to enter and made her way into the burned-out shell of the building that had once been her home.

The spent embers and broken glass crunched under her feet like a crust of newly formed ice. As she walked through the remains of the house, it was difficult to tell exactly where she was. It was as if the fire had altered the entire layout, mischievously moving rooms and putting them in places they hadn't been before.

A bolt of panic raced through her—what if the thing she was looking for was gone? Smashed or melted or somehow destroyed by the relentless flames?

Eventually she found a landmark that brought her closer to what she was searching for. The glass-fronted china cabinet that had stood in her hallway was still there, or rather, what remained of it. It had fallen over during the fire and the glass doors had shattered, spilling most of the plates and collectibles onto the charred floor. Many had shattered, but some of the things, miraculously, were only chipped or cracked. Some had survived unscathed except for a layer of thick black soot. Her heart pounding with excitement, Elizabeth dropped to her knees in the cinders, her hands sifting through the shards of porcelain. She became more and more frantic as she realized, to her horror, that what she sought was not to be found there.

Finally, she sat back on her heels and groaned. "Where is it?" she said aloud. "Where is Bethie's angel?"

She closed her eyes tight to think, attempting to re-create those moments just a few hours earlier, a different lifetime before the fire. A glimmer of a memory came to her—she had given the angel to Beth and she had it with her when she went—Elizabeth strained, working her memory like a muscle to remember what had transpired between the two of them. Then, like a white flash in the dark part of her recollection it came to her. She remembered now—she had sent Beth off to watch television in the study.

Elizabeth jumped to her feet and looked around

the blackened room, bewildered for a moment. She couldn't quite make out where the study was exactly. She took a tentative step in one direction then heard a voice behind her.

"Elizabeth?"

As Monica stepped out of the shadows, Elizabeth turned, startled and panicked. Monica was holding Beth's porcelain angel in her hands. She was dressed in spotless white and there seemed to be a warm glow shimmering around her.

"What . . . what are you doing here?" Her voice was filled with the most profound fear.

Monica held out the angel to her. "Is this what you're looking for, Elizabeth?" she asked.

"I . . . ," Elizabeth began. She felt herself start to tremble, as if she were suddenly very cold. "What are you doing here, Monica?"

Monica smiled, a smile that illuminated the burned-out space. "Please, Elizabeth . . . Don't be afraid . . . I am an angel. I was sent to you and I've been with you all this time. There is a purpose in my coming."

Elizabeth's eyes went wide as tiny pieces began to fit into the puzzle, as she began to realize what had happened and what was happening in that moment. "It was you," she gasped. "You did it. You pulled Bethie out of the fire."

Monica nodded. "That's right," she said softly. "What else do you remember about the fire?"

Elizabeth looked down at the blistered and scorched floorboards at her feet. Then the reality closed around her like a cold shroud. "My cigarette . . . ," she said, aghast. "I started it. The whole thing was my fault, wasn't it?"

Monica nodded again. "Yes, you did. It *was* your fault, Elizabeth. The consequences are yours too."

Elizabeth could no longer hide behind her overweening pride, her much-vaunted reputation as a journalist; nor could she hide behind a liquor bottle any longer. Those days, those excuses, had vanished in an instant. When the truth was spoken, it was as if a light were turned on, and everything in the shadows disappeared.

Suddenly Elizabeth was weeping, and she had to fight to draw breath through her sobs.

"Oh, my God," she wailed. Then she sank to her knees on the burned floor. "Oh, my God . . ." She looked up at Monica even though she was almost blinded by her tears. The expression on Elizabeth's face suggested that she was now awaiting a terrible judgment. "You've been sent here to punish me, haven't you? That's why you're here, isn't it?"

Monica shook her head and knelt down in front of Elizabeth, the smile on her face making her whole being shine. She held the little angel out in front of her.

"No, Elizabeth," she said softly. "No . . . I've come to tell you that God loves you." Then, with great reverence, she put the angel in Elizabeth's hands.

Elizabeth looked down at it as though it were the most precious and prestigious award she had ever won. Then she asked the question she had been waiting to ask her whole life.

"Why?" she asked. "Why would God love a terrible person like me? The things I've done . . . The people I've hurt . . ." She shook her head, suddenly taking stock of her misspent life. How could she have been so wrong for so long?

"Why does God love you?" said Monica. "Because you're Elizabeth, not Elizabeth the globe-trotting journalist or the winner of the Pulitzer prize . . . or even the wretched alcoholic. But because you're you." Monica put her hand out to Elizabeth. "God loves *you*, Elizabeth," she said. "And who you are today is not who you were created to be, the real you is someone else."

"I . . . I don't think I understand," Elizabeth stammered. "I'm not sure—"

Monica did her best to explain. "You spent your whole life running and running, trying to catch up with something or someone that was never there for you."

Elizabeth nodded. It was beginning to make sense to her now. She spent her whole life chasing a brass ring trying to prove herself to the boys' club and the rest of the world.

"But all you've managed to do," Monica continued, "is move farther and farther away from the precious love that is always there for you." Monica sighed and there were tears in her eyes now. She was weeping because the mercy of God was so great. "And now you've almost lost that love completely."

Monica's words hit Elizabeth hard and she broke down, doubling over with gut-wrenching sobs. "I'm so sorry," she managed to gasp through her tears. "I'm sorry . . ." Her face was almost touching the floor, her tears mixing with the ashes. "God, forgive me, I'm so sorry . . . What am I going to do?"

Monica leaned down and put a comforting hand on her back. "Elizabeth," she whispered. "You just did it. You asked for forgiveness . . ." She took her by the shoulders and sat her up straight, looking into her tear-streaked face. She smiled at her, as if giving her courage.

"Now," said Monica, "gather yourself up. You know what you have to do."

Elizabeth looked down at the angel in her hands and nodded. "Yes, I know," she said.

Sydney had stretched out on the hospital bed next to Beth and had fallen asleep alongside her daughter, exhausted by the events of the day. She managed to fall asleep despite the beeps and clicks of the machines that were keeping her daughter alive.

Sydney was in such a deep sleep that she didn't even hear Elizabeth and Monica enter the room. Neither did she hear her mother cross the room to stand near the bed and turn the clockwork key in the base of the porcelain angel music box. Elizabeth set it down on the bedside table before she and Monica quietly left the room. As the door was closing, the soft, golden notes of

"Amazing Grace" began tinkling out near Beth's ear.

Beth continued in her coma, the oxygen mask clamped on her face. But as the music began to fill the room, Beth shifted slightly and her eyelids started to flutter. By the time "Amazing Grace" began playing for the third time, Beth's eyelids trembled again, and then she opened her eyes wide, blinking in astonishment at what she was seeing. She tried to speak but the mask prevented her getting out a word.

Sydney sat bolt upright. "Beth? *Bethie!*" For a moment she did not dare to hope, but it was obvious. Her daughter had emerged from her coma, and she was responding to the familiar music.

Sydney jumped off the bed. "Nurse!" she called. "Nurse! Please, come quickly!"

For years she would call Beth's sudden and astonishing recovery a "miracle"—but she would always know that it had been a miracle from God, brought to them through her mother . . .

Chapter Twelve

The evening session at the New Hope Center had already begun when Monica and Elizabeth quietly came in through the door at the back of the hall. There were about forty people there already sitting in rows of folding chairs, some of them drinking coffee. Elizabeth had decided she was going to make a clean sweep of it.

As she had said to Monica on the way over, "If I'm going to be healthy . . . I might as well be really healthy . . ."

Anita was running the meeting, standing at the podium facing the group, but she wasn't speaking when Monica and Elizabeth entered. Rather, a professional-looking man was standing and addressing the others.

". . . So I just wanted to say how much I appreciate coming here—after only a month, it has really made a difference and I just want to say thanks." He shrugged and smiled. "So thank you."

"Thank you, David," said Anita. She led the applause as the man sat down in his place.

Monica and Elizabeth stopped far behind the last row of chairs. Elizabeth would have to make the rest of the journey on her own. Monica took Elizabeth's hand and folded it between both of hers. She leaned forward and whispered in her ear. "I know you can do it, Elizabeth," she said. "I know God has given you the strength . . ."

Elizabeth said nothing, just nodded and smiled. The truth of it was she didn't feel the strength. She had never been so terrified in her entire life. She took a deep breath and left Monica at the back of the hall, walking toward the last row of seats.

Anita noticed her as she was taking a seat, but said nothing; nor did she gesture. It was a sovereign rule of the meetings that members did not speak and did not seek acknowledgment until they were absolutely ready to do so. It was strictly up to them to decide when to tell the group about their problems with alcohol.

"So," Anita said brightly, "do we have any newcomers tonight who would like to introduce themselves? All you have to do is say your first name and anything else about yourself that you feel comfortable sharing with us . . ."

A burly, red-bearded young man sitting directly in front of Elizabeth raised his hand and stood up.

"Go ahead," said Anita.

"My name's Barry . . . ," he began. Elizabeth, right behind him, could feel the young man's nervousness, which was reflected in his voice.

"Hi, Barry," the entire group answered.

Barry swallowed hard. "Hi . . . actually, this isn't my first time here, it's my second. The first time I just sat in the back and didn't say anything at all."

Elizabeth thought, *That is a very wise course of action, Barry*. It was something Elizabeth planned on doing herself. It wasn't that she was not committed to sobriety—she finally was—but she wanted to get the hang of things at these meetings first.

"I came back this week . . ." Barry stopped, as if unsure of what to say next. "I'm just back . . . that's all." He shrugged. "That's all I can do right now." Barry sat down abruptly.

"Thank you, Barry," said Anita. "We're glad you're here. We're glad you came back . . ." She looked around the room. "Are there any other newcomers? Is there anyone else who would like to say something here?" The room was silent. And Elizabeth sat firmly rooted to her seat. She was not ready to speak.

"Okay . . . ," said Anita, moving the meeting along. "Well, I think we have some birthdays to celebrate today." In the recovery movement "birthdays" were celebrations of sobriety and were coveted triumphs for each and every member. "So," said Anita, "who has a birthday today? Who wants to go first?"

Elizabeth was not watching the room, but had her eyes down, lost in thought. She did not see the young woman stand up and walk to the front of the room. But she heard what she said:

"Hi," she said, "my name is Sydney and I'm an alcoholic."

"Hi, Sydney," the group responded.

Elizabeth looked up and her eyes grew wide as she caught sight of her daughter standing in front of the group. The words "I'm an alcoholic" seemed to echo in the air.

Sydney nodded and smiled. "As of today I have been sober for exactly a year."

"All right!" someone shouted and there was long and enthusiastic applause from the group. When the clapping died down, Sydney nodded and began to speak.

"I used to say that I was an alcoholic because

my mother didn't love me . . ." Elizabeth knew Sydney had no idea she was in the room.

"But I realized that it wasn't that my mother didn't love me," Sydney went on. "Nothing changed until I admitted that I was an alcoholic because I didn't love myself . . . I used to think that my mother was so glamorous. She was always jetting off to the most exotic places . . . she would meet the most famous people . . . and drink champagne from crystal glasses from Paris." Sydney paused and shook her head slowly. "I adored her. I was so *proud* of her . . ."

Elizabeth was hearing all this for the first time. It had never dawned on her that her daughter would have felt this way. But then again, Elizabeth had spent most of her busy life thinking only about herself.

"I adored her . . . But I always knew," Sydney went on, "in my heart, I *knew* that she was sorry she had me. I guess I . . . I guess I cramped her style."

Sydney's sincere and candid words caused

pain to shoot through the center of Elizabeth's body. It was a pain buried deep in her soul.

Sydney shrugged. "So I . . . I tried to make her happy that I was born. I drew her pictures. I . . . I sent her letters while she was on the road . . ." Sydney tried to keep her voice steady but with the painful memories came the tears. "I tried so hard to be somebody that she could love . . . But I couldn't compete with the champagne."

Elizabeth sat stock-still, not daring to move. The room was silent; everyone's attention was focused on her daughter.

"And the harder I tried," Sydney continued, "the more I saw myself through my mother's eyes: I thought she saw a dull, unexciting little girl. Uninteresting and stupid, I guess. So why should she bother with me? Who could blame her for choosing to go off on exciting trips instead of staying at home with me?"

She sighed and wiped her eyes. "And then one day I'm pouring a . . . drink for myself in the afternoon—I'm not drunk yet, but I know I will be—when my little girl comes into the house and she looks at me and out of nowhere she says, 'Mommy . . . I'm so glad that you were born.'"

There was a little catch in Sydney's voice as the tears started again. But this time she was crying tears of joy. "And finally . . . finally . . . for the first time in my life . . . so was I. I was happy I was alive—I had never felt that way before."

A huge surge of sorrow coursed through Elizabeth, followed by an even greater wave of love for her daughter. She wanted to reach out to this poor young woman, hold her in her arms, comfort her. She wanted to make her life happy. Elizabeth, overcome by maternal love, was not even aware that she was standing up, gazing at her daughter.

It took a moment for the sight to register with Sydney. This was—quite literally—the last place she expected to see her mother suddenly appear.

"Mom?" she said, scarcely able to believe her eyes. "What are you—"

"Sydney . . . ," said Elizabeth softly, gently. "I am so sorry . . ." There were tears in her eyes too. "And I am *so* glad you were born . . . Please believe that. It's the truth."

Sydney was so moved she could not speak. She nodded and fought back her tears.

"And happy birthday, darling," said Elizabeth. "Do you mind sharing it with me?"

"No," Sydney managed to say. "No."

Then, as if suddenly aware of all the eyes in the room focused on her, Elizabeth looked around at the other members gathered there. Many of them had tears glistening on their faces too—every single person there had gone through some kind of emotional upheaval—something that had driven them to seek recovery and support.

Elizabeth smiled wanly and wiped her eyes. This was what her whole life had come down to. All the struggle and strife, all the adventures and escapades, the pleasure and the pain, the wars and the world leaders—the rivers of alcohol she had consumed since her earliest years—the sum of the experiences of her life had come down to this one moment.

Sydney's eyes were shining—with tears? With pride? Probably a combination of both. Elizabeth stood up straight. She had reached rock bottom, and yet somehow, that's where she finally found the strength Monica had promised. In a clear voice she said: "My name is Elizabeth. And I'm an alcoholic."

"Hi, Elizabeth," said the group.

Very quietly, at the back of the hall, Monica stood up and left the room.

Tess was sitting behind the wheel of her enormous red Cadillac convertible, the engine idling, when Monica emerged from the New Hope Center. She could tell by the bright, shining look on Monica's face that her assignment had been a successful one.

Monica slid into the passenger seat and heaved a great sigh of relief. "Well, that's done," she said.

"Any marimba playing going on in there?" Tess asked. There was a mischievous smile on her face as she spoke.

Monica shook her head. "No. But there's beautiful music, Tess. Beautiful music."

Tess put the big car in drive. "That'll be some interesting book of memoirs she's going to write," she said. She took her foot off the brake and the great red behemoth began to roll downhill.

Monica nodded in agreement. "Aye," she said. "I think it will be worth waiting for."

"It always is, Baby," said Tess, laughing. "It always is."